THE
ARITHMETIC
OF GOD

CONTAINING THE NUMBERS
OF THE HOLY BIBLE

AUTHORIZED KING JAMES VERSION

FROM ONE TO 666

and

INFALLIBLE PROOFS
FROM THE WORD OF GOD

Penning Scribe: Don Kistler

AUTHOR:
JESUS CHRIST THE WORD

The Gates of Praise Lighthouse
BOOK & CASSETTE TAPE MINISTRIES
1830 Broadway   Tel. 252-8385
Everett, Washington Zip 98201

First Printing 1976 — 5000 Copies

Printed in the United States of America

For Additional Copies
Write P.O. Box 573
Kings Mountain, North Carolina 28086

Inclose $3.00
(Plus 50¢ for Handling and Mailing)

Foreword

This book was given by inspiration of the Holy Ghost, the Author is the Alpha and Omega. His name is Yeshua, Salvation, Jesus Christ by Which all things were created, for He is the I am, Father, Son and Holy Ghost. The Author brings forth the Word of God so really that the truth comes to revelation and leads one to know that the Spirit cannot be seen, but Jesus Christ is the Spirit. The Living Word of God becomes alive and reveals Himself as Spirit and Truth and shall come again in Glory. Words can be changed and given private interpretation but numbers remain the same in all languages and dialects. The Author did not put all of His Word into this book, but enough of it to convince the reader that *The Arithmetic of God* will bring on a unity of the faith which is Spirit and Truth.

This is not some commentary of the Word of God, but is infallible proof that men of God, written with the mind of Jehovah. The scribe who penned this book has only written what the audible voice of God revealed to him, no more and no less. What God reveals to you by this revelation will be the knowledge and wisdom of God Jehovah, Jesus Christ, it will not be of man. Don Kistler, a Jew completed, is the scribe of this revelation hid since the foundation of the world for this end time generation. If you wish to come against this work of

God Jesus Christ, then on Judgment day it will reveal its truth as you pass from death unto life, or death unto death. The scribe may say only One be true, the Word of God and every man be a liar. That which is scripture is God, and that which is not is of man. "All scripture is given inspiration of God, and is profitable for doctrine, for reproof, for correction, for instruction in righteousness, that the man of God may be perfect, throughly furnished unto all good works." (II Timothy 3:16 & 17)

May all your days be blessed with the seven Spirits of God. Isaiah 11:1-5: "And there shall come forth a rod out of the stem of Jesse, and a Branch shall grow out of his roots: And the spirit of the (1) *Lord* shall rest upon him, the spirit of (2) *wisdom* and (3) *understanding*, the spirit of (4) *counsel* and (5) *might*, the *spirit* of (6) *knowledge* and of the (7) *fear of the Lord*; And shall make him of quick understanding in the fear of the Lord: and he shall not judge after the sight of his eyes, neither reprove after the hearing of his ears: But with righteousness shall he judge the poor, and reprove with equity for the meek of the earth: and he shall smite the earth with the rod of his mouth, and with the breath of his lips shall he slay the wicked. And righteousness shall be the girdle of his loins, and faithfulness the girdle of his reins."

A Word About the Scribe

At the publishing of this book Brother Don Kistler is 52 years of age, a completed Jew born in Indianapolis, Indiana, of Jewish parents, Hilda Yho and Don Kistler, and has one sister, Patrica Bear. He is married and has five children. Don is a called man of God — not by religion or organization, but by the will of the living God Jehovah. He was completed through the washing of regeneration and renewing of the Holy Ghost. (Titus 3:5) And by this entered into the Kingdom of God. (John 3:5 and Acts 2:38)

Don received a personal experience through Jesus Christ, heard the audible voice of God speak and reveal a revelation hid from the foundation of the world. The Lord spoke and said, "I will make you my prophet unto all nations unto the Jew first, and also to the Greek, for my Word will be sure; Yeshua, Salvation, unto all that enter into the Kingdom of God."

He has stated in the foreword of the book that he is not the Author, but the scribe, who penned it all down as God Jehovah revealed it to him in a building in Denver, Colorado, while fasting and praying away from his family during a nine-month period.

Don wishes that only his Jesus be lifted up, that the Spirit be drawn unto you the Lord of your Yeshua, Salvation.

Don said, "I am not God, I am only His son; he that worships God worships him in Spirit and Truth. The Lord will reveal truth by His unchangeable Numbers which I call *The Arithmetic of God*." Faith pleases God.

Don is dedicated to his Father Jehovah. He is always glad to speak before any group by the leading of the Holy Spirit of God; you may write him as long as he lives in this world through this address: Mr. Don Kistler, P.O. Box 573, Kings Mountain, North Carolina 28086.

Table of Contents

Introduction

I'm going to bring you in this book something I've been promising to the people who have known me for a long time: The Revelation of the Bible Numbers. A Revelation which I received from the Lord Jesus Christ, through His Power and for His Glory. I want them to be known by all those who seek to know the Word of God in Power, for I believe that numbers have a lot to do with the Power and understanding of the Word of God, for Jesus told me it would open up the revelation of truth of the Holy Bible. Yes, I believe it to be very, very important.

A few years ago here at God's Community Church of Charity, located at 1345 South Dayton Street in Denver, Colorado, the Lord gave me a Revelation of this that led to a study of the numbers connected with the Bible and the Tabernacle. This has opened up a field of study and it opened up a Revelation from Jesus Christ. And it has become more miraculous day by day. In various places I've taught the Bible from every standpoint. This in turn has brought about, from my having mentioned the numbers many times, that I bring forth this teaching. But first I felt that I must have a complete Revelation on this, for I believe that for someone to teach, he himself must have this teaching clear in his own mind. I prayed concerning this and Jesus gave me a Revelation of the

1

Numbers contained in the Holy Bible.

The Bible reveals God to be a God of numbers. The Psalmist said of the Lord, "He telleth the number of the stars; he calleth them all by their names." That's in Psalm 147:4. The modern telescopes show that there are millions of stars reaching out into space and so infinite that men do not have numerical figures sufficient to measure their distances. Yet the word of God tells us the number of these stars and "calleth them all by name." Job said, "For now thou numberest my steps:" You'll find that in Job 14:16. If it were so in the case of Job, is it not so in the case of all people? When we think of all the steps taken by all the men who ever lived and then realize that God numbered them all, then we can better understand the words of the Psalmist when he said, "Great is our Lord, and of great power: his understanding is infinite." That's Psalm 147:5. Again Job said, "Seeing his days are determined, the number of his months are with thee." That's found in Job 14:5. Jesus said that not a sparrow could fall to the ground without the Father's notice and that the very hair of the heads of his people are all numbered. That's found in Matthew 10:29, 30. And when we think of all of the many sparrows that have fallen to the earth and the countless billions of hairs that have been on the heads of people since time began and how the number of hairs on different heads are changing from day to day then we can indeed see, hallelujah, how our God is a God of numbers and that His knowledge is infinite. Jesus said, concerning the law, "Till heaven and earth pass, one jot or one tittle shall in no wise pass from the law till all be fulfilled," (Matthew 5:18) Every word and every letter in the Word of God was in His mind before a line of it was ever written. The numbers within the Word were known to Him before they were penned. This shall be seen as I go into the numbers with you in this book. Indeed, our God is great and infinite in His understanding.

There are many incidents in the Bible Arithmetic of God showing evidence of the numerical design which runs through the Scriptures. For instance, the distance around the Tabernacle was 300 cubits. "The length of the court shall be an hundred cubits, and the breadth fifty every where," That's found in Exodus 27:18. Now, the two long sides were 100 cubits each, the two ends were 50 cubits each. Two times 100 plus two times 50 equals 300 cubits. In this Court was the Altar which was five cubits wide while four cubits square. "And the height thereof shall be three cubits." (Exodus 27:1) The product of the number connected with the Altar is 300, the number of cubits around the Court. Five times five is 25, four times 25 is 100 and three times 100 is 300. On this Altar within the Court the Priest offered the sacrifice. In I Chronicles, the 24th chapter, verses 1-19, there are found 24 divisions of the Priesthood. These are the divisions of the sons of Aaron, Nadab, Abihu, Eleazar and Ithamar. Among the sons of Eleazar there were 16 chief men of the house of their fathers and eight among the sons of Ithamar. Sixteen and eight make 24. When all the numbers from one to 24 are added the sum is 300, the number of cubits around the court. Noah's ark was 300 cubits long. The distance around the Court of the Tabernacle, the length of the ark shall be 300 cubits, and the breadth of it 50 cubits and the height of it 30 cubits. See Genesis 6:15. Thus the length of the ark was the same as the distance around the Court of the Tabernacle. The Tabernacle itself was 30 cubits long, which was the height of Noah's ark. It was made of boards standing up which were a cubit and a half wide. That's found in Exodus 26:15, 16. The long side had 20 boards each on the south side pointing southward. That's in Exodus 26:18. The north side likewise 20 boards. See Exodus 26:20. Twenty times one and one half cubits equals 30 cubits which was the length of the Tabernacle and also the height of Noah's ark. From the time God told Noah to make the ark until Noah and all in the ark came out the ark is mentioned 24 times. Those places are listed for you to read. The places the ark is mentioned until all in the ark came out are: Twice in Genesis 6:14, 6:15 and 6:16 again in 6:16, 6:18, 6:19, 7:1, 7:7, 7:9, 7:13, 7:15, 7:17, 7:18, 7:23, 8:1, 8:4, 8:6, 8:9, again in 8:9, 8:10, 8:13, 8:16, 8:19.

Now the total of these is 300 cubits, the length of the ark if you add one to 24 inclusive.

Another example is in John 21:11-14, where there is a record of the disciples catching 153 fish. That day Jesus showed Himself to them for the third time since His Resurrection. His Resurrection took place on the 17th day of the month. He was crucified on the Passover or 14th day and rose three days later. When all the numbers from one to 17 are added, they total 153, the number of fish caught. When the 17 is multiplied by the three again for the third time Jesus showed Himself after His Resurrection, the product is 153. Seventeen times three times three equals 153. This is another of the wonderful things to be learned through the numerology of the Bible! And why is it wonderful? Because, as in all things, it shows the perceiving mind the hidden beauty, wisdom and intelligent strength of God.

Israel was saved out of Egypt's bondage the night of the Passover. This you will find in Exodus 12:24-42. And all the numbers from one to 14 add up to 105. This number was connected with the birth of Enos at whose birth men began to call upon the name of the Lord.

In his discussion of justification by faith, Romans 3:22 through 5:2, Paul uses the word "faith" 19 times and the numbers from one to 19 add up to 190, the combined ages of Abraham and Sarah when Isaac was born. In Hebrews 11:11 it is stated, "Through faith also Sarah herself received strength to conceive seed, and was delivered of a child when she was past age," In Genesis 17:1-21, the Lord appeared unto Abraham when he was 99 years old and told him at a set time the next year that Sarah would give birth to Isaac. Abraham said, "Shall a child be born to him that is a hundred years old and shall Sarah that is ninety years old bear?" Genesis 21:5 says, "And Abraham was a hundred years old, when his son Isaac was born unto him." So Abraham was 100 years old and Sarah was 90 years old when Isaac was born. Thus the combined ages of the two parents equal 190 years. It was through faith that this birth was brought about. The

4

number 19 stands for Faith and the numbers from one to 19 add up to 190, the combined ages of the two parents of Isaac. The 19 places Paul uses the word "faith" in discussing justification by faith are Romans 3:22, 3:25, 3:27, 3:28, twice in 3:30, 3:31, 4:5, 4:9, 4:11, 4:12, 4:13, 4:14, twice in 4:16, 4:19, 4:20, 5:1 and the 19th time in 5:2.

I say I received this Revelation from Jesus Christ. I don't intend to make any mistakes. Praise God. Now, the total is 190 if you add the numbers from one to 19 together. That is the combined ages of Abraham and Sarah when Isaac was born. In Genesis 17:23 it is stated that Ishmael, Abraham's son by the bondswoman, was circumcised when 13 years old. In Genesis 21:4 it is stated that Isaac, Abraham's second-born son was circumcised when eight days old. The difference between 13 and eight is five which number shall be seen to stand for Grace. In Genesis 21:5 we find that Isaac was born when Abraham was 100 years old. Israel was saved out of bondage on the 14th day of the month. In this case it has been shown that five is the difference between the numbers connected with Ishmael and Isaac, which numbers are eight and 13. When you take eight from 13 you get five. There was a difference of 14 years in their birth. When these two numbers, five and 14, are added they total 19, the number connected with Faith.

Now, let us read Ephesians 2:8 and use the numeral value of Grace, Salvation and Faith. By Grace (5) are ye saved (Salvation — 14) through Faith (19). Number five for Grace plus 14 for Salvation add up to 19 for Faith. Now the sum of three numbers five, 14, and 19 add up to 38. It is seen also that the numbers from one to 19 add up to 190, which, you will recall, is the combined ages of Abraham and Sarah at Isaac's birth. And when 190 is divided by five, the difference between the numbers connected with the circumcision of Ishmael and Isaac, we get exactly 38, the same number we get by adding five, 14 and 19. Later on the beauty and glory of all this will be seen of all these numbers. The three numbers that are connected with the circumcision are: Abraham

5

was circumcised when he was 99 years old, Ishmael at the age of 13 years and Isaac at eight days. We find this in the 99 years of Abraham in Genesis 17:24, Ishmael as 13 years old in Genesis 17:25 and Isaac on the eighth day in Genesis 21:4. Now let us take 13, the number connected with Ishmael and all the numbers from one to 13 and we get 91. To this number 91 add eight, the number connected with Isaac's circumcision and we get 99, the number connected with Abraham's circumcision.

I will bring out the meaning of all this as we study the numbers. This should be enough to convince you that there is a numeral design in the Holy Bible, but this is just a start. I wish to refer to the original language, in Luke 13:16, "And ought not this woman, being a daughter of Abraham, whom Satan hath bound, lo, these eighteen years be loosed from this bond on the Sabbath day?" In this question Jesus asked there are exactly 25 Greek words. The woman was bound 18 years and loosed on the Sabbath or seventh day. The numbers 18 and seven add up to 25, the exact number of Greek words found in the question. In the words, "lo, these eighteen years" there are 18 Greek letters corresponding with the 18 years the woman had been bound. She was loosed on the seventh day and there are just seven letters in the Greek verb "be loosed." In the 17th chapter of Revelation John is shown the judgment of the great whore. She is called a woman six times. (Revelation 17:3, 17:4, 17:6, 17:7, 17:9 and 17:18) Where the woman is mentioned the fifth time we read, "And here is the mind that hath wisdom, the seven heads are seven mountains on which the woman sitteth." In Revelation 17:9 there are 19 Greek letters in the statement, "and here is the mind that hath wisdom." The 19 letters are followed by the statement about seven heads and seven mountains and the woman is mentioned the fifth time. These numbers seven, seven and five add up to 19, the number of Greek letters in the opening statement. Oh, I hope you're getting a Revelation! I sure did. There is no one, after this, who could ever disprove the Bible, that it is not the Word of God in its exactness!

There are hundreds of examples like this that could be given but I believe that this is enough for the present. Now that it is evident that there is a numeral system and design that runs throughout the Bible, the question arises, "How did it happen to be there?" In the first place man would have never thought of fixing a book like this and, in the second place, it would have been impossible for him to make a record that covers thousands of years of time and make the record fit together and word together in such a fashion. In the third place, the various books of the Bible written by many writers, most of whom never saw the others yet always agreeing in the significance of their numbers and as to what each number meant, is staggering. The divine mind was in the whole thing and He Who knew all things from the beginning guided each writer with an unerring hand. If you've ever been in any doubt that the Holy Bible is not truly the Word of God, then when I'm through with this book on this question, I am sure you will be convinced beyond a shadow of a doubt, if you've allowed yourself to get in the Spirit of God and the Holy Ghost, that the Holy Bible is indeed the Word of God.

Now that the numeral design has been proven and since it is concluded that God's mind and plan was in it all, other questions should be asked. Did God ever do a useless thing? Did He ever do a thing in vain? If not, then this numeral system had to come to light in God's own time. If it was never used then would this not be something that God did in vain? Since He has put this numeral system in His Word is it not profitable for doctrine, for reproof, for correction and for instructions in righteousness? "That the man of God may be perfect, throughly furnished unto all good words." (II Timothy 2:17) Is it not part of the armor which God has given to His people to better overcome the devil and the power of darkness? See Ephesians 6:11, 12.

A lot of people ask me, why did God place the system of numbers in the Bible? Well, when we stop to think on the matter it is the most reasonable thing in the world for God to have used this number system in His revelation to man. God told me that this was very significant. God is an unchanging Spirit. The Bible says that He changeth not, "For I am the Lord: I change not." See Malachi 3:6. "Jesus Christ, the same yesterday and today and for ever." See Hebrews 13:8. The science of numbers is an unchanging and unchangeable science. Numbers, and their meaning to men, have always been the same and always will be. Two and two make four and always will. Two and two have never made five nor can they. The science of numbers is a science that has been understood alike by all people in all lands and every age. If any man in any country was asked to put 15 cattle in three pens and the same number in each pen, he would have five in each pen. So what better system could the unchangeable God use to reveal Himself and His unchangeable truth than the unchangeable science of numbers? Words change and their meaning and usage change as time goes by but the numbers, like God, never change.

God associated different numbers with different doctrines and things. Sin has its number and there is a number for death and a number for eternal life, there is a number for the Resurrection and for Redemption. And there's a number for Judgment and there's a number for Salvation. And all these shall be found in due time as I bring forth the numbers to you, children of God. I pray God that many gather together to read this, for it's not only interesting, but it will give you a revelation. It will open your whole mind to a new understanding. It will give you a new meaning to the Holy Bible.

What is, really, the value of knowing the system of numbers? Well, the question is sometimes asked of me, "Just what is the point in all this and of what value would it be to me?" As Paul said in Romans 3:2, "Much every way." Those are the words that come to my mind. First of all, it gives the servant of God an invincible weapon with which to meet all modernists, infidels, agnostics and atheists. The combined wisdom of the world cannot begin to make an argument against this system of numbers. We need not fear the unbelieving, unsaved professor, or scoffing infidels any longer. They must stand forever confounded before the evidence of Bible numbers. Thank You, Jesus, for bringing it to me. I pray God, in the power of the Holy Ghost, to be with me.

Suppose one has a son or daughter, relative or friend, who has come under the influence of Christ-denying teachers in modernist schools. This number system may be used to fortify them against such influence. They can hand him a book on Bible numbers to read and that will put the dunce cap on him. Every pastor, Sunday School teacher, personal worker and every parent should prepare themselves to help immature students over these hard places in their lives. God has put within our hands a weapon with which we can make a laughingstock of those who set themselves to be opposed to the Word of God. Oh, thank You, Jesus! I think that there's only a short time left until He comes, and I must do everything I can to bring forth the truth, for you must worship Him in Spirit and in Truth.

The third thing is a knowledge of the Bible system of numbers will enable one to better understand the Bible for himself. An application of the Bible numbers brings out the meaning of the Tabernacle as never before. The doctrine of grace, redemption, faith and the new birth, divine power, security, the resurrection, Israel's conversion and restoration, the millennial rain are all made to shine out in such a way as to make the believer's heart leap with joy. It was through these numbers, children of God, that I came into this revelation of Jesus Christ and of His coming. When you know them, doubtful passages will be cleared up for any Bible student. For example, there has long been a difference of opinion about the passage, "There is a sin unto death." See I John 5:16. Some have contended that it refers to the physical death of a child of God. Others have insisted that it refers to a lost man. An application of the Bible numbers clears up its meaning. Some have insisted that the first resurrection of Revelation 20:4-8 is a new birth; others that it will be a bodily resurrection of the saved dead. The number for the new birth is not found in that passage. On the other hand the number three, which is the Bible number for the resurrection of the body of Christ and His people is found in that passage. The third time the 1000 years is mentioned is where John said, "They lived and reigned with Christ 1000 years." Then John goes on to say, "This is the first resurrection." This ties up the number three for the resurrection and the 1000 years reign in the same connection. This will become plainer as I go on with you in this revelation of numbers.

Now the fourth reason is that a study of the Bible system of numbers will give one the most profound respect for the wisdom of God and for the immeasurable greatness of God's word. Often, I, as I studied and received this revelation, was made to stop and marvel at the greatness of our God, of Jesus Christ, Who was God, Who is God, the one God. It has always been taught that God was all wise and that He knew the end from the beginning, and since I have been made to see how God could and did devise a system of numbers that fits into the birth, life and experience of Bible characters in such a way as to picture all His plans, purposes and dealings with men from time eternal, then indeed I have been made to marvel and bow in humility before the immeasurable greatness of God. I claim to be only a servant and a son of God, Jesus Christ, the one God Almighty for I know His greatness. I fear the Lord Jesus Christ.

The fifth reason is that this is a part of the believer's armor by which he is to overcome all in his conflict with Satan and the powers of darkness. In these days when the world is being swamped with books and tracts put out by atheist and communist men high in scholarship and learning, training their batteries on the Word of God, we need the knowledge of these numbers as never before. Mordecai said to Esther, "Who knoweth whether thou art come to the kingdom for such a time as this?" See Esther 4:14. Who knows but that God placed this hidden wisdom in His Word, "for such a time as this?" I don't know any preachers who have ever brought forth this revelation. I never really had an understanding of it until Jesus Christ gave me that understanding, and what a revelation it was, what an understanding it became, what a need I had for it! In all the years I studied Judaism, Catholicism, the Bible, in all the years I studied after I became a full Gospel non-denominational, one in Jesus Christ, I had no idea the numerology was there. But then God brought forth the revelation. It gave me an understanding, to almost the week, of His coming. I know many things by these numbers. In this book I promise to connect fundamental doctrine in the Word of God to the numerology of the Bible. The Divine Authority and Inspiration of the scriptures will be shown with numbers and Bible numbers, along with quotations. The virgin birth of Jesus Christ will be connected upon, Blood and redemption will be shown to be in the Bible system of numbers. The resurrection of Jesus and His people will be connected with the number three about 100 times and when all the numbers are brought to collaborate the positive statement of the great truth of the Word, the Bible critics will be at their wit's end. They can no longer escape by saying that the Bible writers are only setting forth their personal views. He will also have this vast unerring number system to account for, except by admitting that it is the work of God. Children of God, I would like to get started now to bring forth the significance of various numbers, but before I go into each individual number I will give diligently to the study of the parts of the works of numbers. I believe that you will find them fascinating and gripping.

One young preacher who has been taught this number system said, "It is something that gets hold of a person and will not let him go." Many preachers are already pursuing this line of study in the most profitable way. Do not say you cannot learn it. If you are a child of God and have just average intelligence you can learn it. People in every walk of life whose education is very limited are memorizing the numbers and what they signify. They are learning to study the Bible by this method. The hard work has already been done. You will be made to see how it all fits together through the revelation of Jesus Christ and the power of the Holy Ghost, if you are willing to seek the Spirit of God.

It has already been stated that six is Satan's number, not only by me but by others. The serpent who beguiled Eve and the tool of Satan was the sixth character in the Bible. The first three — the Father, the Word of Jesus, and the Holy Ghost — are followed by Adam, Eve and finally the serpent. The devil shall be traced by this number from one end of the Bible to the other. And when God had finished His creative work He rested on the seventh day. This number is connected with completion throughout the Bible. After the account of the completed work of God, there is given an account of the transgression brought by Satan through the serpent, and when six, Satan's number, is added to seven, the number connected with the completed work of creation, the sum is 13, the number connected with sin, rebellion, transgression and the fallen nature of man from one end of the Bible to the other.

When man became a sinner, represented by the number 13, he was in need of Salvation from sin, and the next number is 14, and it is the number connected with Salvation. Israel was saved from Egyptian bondage on the 14th day of the first month. That's found in Exodus 12:18-27. There was a 14-year difference in the time of the birth of Ishmael, Abraham's firstborn son, and in the birth of Isaac, his second-born son. See Genesis 16:16 and 21:5. Salvation, represented by the number 14, makes the difference between those born after the flesh as in Galatians 4:23 and the children of promise as in Galatians 4:28, who have been born the second time. All this is a part of the divine system of numbers. I'm sure you will see the number 12 is for Divine Authority or Power. Note how often the number 12 is connected with the Holy City, the New Jerusalem which shall come down from God out of heaven. Read Revelation 21:1 all the way to 22:2. To go beyond Divine Authority is to sin and become a transgressor. To go beyond 12 is to go to 13, the number for sin and that is why Jesus mentioned 13 evil things which come out of the heart of man and defile him. See Mark 7:21 to 23. Now, the number 11 is one short of 12. To fall one point is to come short of the divine requirement and to come under judgment. Eleven is the number for judgment. God said He would bring Israel out of Egypt by great judgments. That's found in Exodus 7:4. Counting the overthrow of Pharaoh's army at the Red Sea there were 11 judgments of Egypt. The number for the law is ten. There were ten commandments. A broken law calls for judgment. The judgment follows a broken law and he that is guilty in one point is guilty of the whole. See James 2:10. So if one has broken one of the ten commandments then the whole law is charged against him and judgment is due to fall. So 11 for Judgment which comes after ten which is the law is logical.

This judgment must be pronounced by divine authority and 12 is the next number after 11. When Judgment is passed by Divine Authority, the penalty is death. In Romans 1:29 to 32, Paul lists 23 evil things which men do and say. "Such are worthy of death"; and thereby come under judgment of God. When 12 for Divine Authority is added to 11 for judgment, the total is 23, the exact number of things Paul lists in this connection. In Numbers 15:32-36, a man was stoned to death for picking up sticks on the Sabbath or the seventh day of the week. The commandment concerning the Sabbath was the fourth. Now, in Exodus 20:8-9, seven plus four makes 11, the number for judgment. And the man brought judgment upon himself by violation of the fourth commandment which concerns the seventh day. Four plus seven equals 11. This judgment was pronounced by God Himself (Verse 10). The 12 is the number for divine authority. When this 12 is added to 11, (four plus seven) the sum is 23, the number for death. It has already been stated that 13 is the number for sin and ten for the law. In I Corinthians 15:56 it is stated, "The sting of death is sin; and the strength of sin is the law." This verse shows that sin, working through the law, brings death. The ten, the number for the Law is added to 13, the number for sin, the sum is 23, the number for death.

From this we can see the right words and the right numeral values always come around at the right time to fit with precision. Who but God could design such a number system and fix such a book that brings the right number around at the right time and place? Praise God and give glory to His precious name!

In Esther 9:1-10, it is seen that Haman's ten sons were put to death on the 13th day of the month and these two numbers ten and 13 added together total 23, the number for death. This is just a sample, children, of how the Bible numbers work together and I'm going to open to you this whole revelation through the power of the Holy Ghost. They not only add but they subtract, divide and multiply. For example three, the number for the Resurrection, subtracted from 23 for death leaves 20, the number for Redemption, as in Romans 8:23. In Exodus 30:12-14, the males in Israel paid ransom or redemption money from the age of 20 years and upward. Boaz redeemed the property of three dead men, Elinelech, Chilion and Mehlon. That's found in Ruth 4:1-10. It's found 20 times in the book of Ruth. Boaz married Ruth, the widow of Mahlon, the third mentioned, to raise up the name of the dead upon his inheritance. Here we have redemption and Boaz's name is found 20 times in the book of Ruth. We have the raising up the name of the dead and it is seen that there were three of them and here's the number three for the resurrection. When 20 and three are added the sum is 23 for death. The number system is perfect in every way. The Bible doesn't change, only men try to change the Bible. It always fits together to form a perfect picture.

Now there's another thought here and I might as well give it to you right now as the Holy Ghost reveals it to mind. People say that men put the Bible together in chapter and in verse. They did, but only by the help of God. I don't take any other version of the Bible except the King James, unless of course it would be the original manuscripts, which are not available to anyone.

So, children of God, I'm going to start now to give you the

revelation that Jesus Christ gave to me, and I pray God, Oh Father in heaven, that every one who reads this book from this day forward will come into all the numbers in the study of Your precious Word, Father, and that they will see by this numeral system, Jesus, that You are the God of all gods. And that You performed the very act of putting it together in its perfection, for You are perfect, You are God, You are the only God, the one God, which is proven in the Holy Word of God through the power of the Holy Ghost, Jesus Christ of Nazareth, as the God of gods, the Father, the Son and the Holy Ghost. Amen.

Unity
"ONE"

Now, the first number would have to be One, because it's in the Beginning. The word UNITY comes from the Latin word "UNUS" meaning "ONE." In the Bible number One stands for UNITY. In John 17:20-22, Jesus prayed for the UNITY of His people. "Neither pray I for these alone, but for them also which shall believe on me through their word; that they all may be one; as thou, Father, art in me, and I in thee, that they also may be one in us: that the world may believe that thou hast sent me. And the glory which thou givest me I have given them; that they may be one, even as we are one:" Jesus was praying that His followers should have one mind, one aim, one objective in life.

The meaning here is harmony, peace and fellowship among them. This is explained in Acts 4:32, "And the multitude of them that believed were of one heart and of one soul". Right after this it is stated, "And with great power gave the Apostles witness of the resurrection of the Lord Jesus: and great grace was upon them all." That's Acts 4:33. It never fails when God's people are of one heart and one soul that great power and grace will rest upon them.

Here it is seen that a great multitude of believers, many in number, all are of one heart, and one soul and one spirit. This is what Jesus meant when He prayed that His people should

16

be one, with one mind, one aim, and one purpose in every respect for He is One God. *Yours Truly* sees no reason for stumbling over the statement that these three are One. No one stumbles over the fact that Jesus prayed for the multitude of His believers to be one as He and the Father were one. If the statement about the Father and the Holy Ghost being one disturbs you, you have the wrong thought. They are but titles to one God. Then since Jesus prayed for as many believers to be one as He and His Father are one, He was wanting them to be as just one person in the Spirit which is the Seven Spirits of God. "And the spirit of the Lord shall rest upon him, the spirit of wisdom and understanding, the spirit of counsel and might, the spirit of knowledge and of the fear of the Lord"; See Isaiah 11:2. Jesus wanted no division among His people. In I Corinthians 1:10, Paul said to the Church at Corinth, "Now I beseech ye brethren, by the name of the Lord Jesus Christ, that ye all speak the same thing, and that there be no divisions among you; but that ye be perfectly joined together in the same mind and in the same judgement". This is what is meant by UNITY.

When Jesus prayed for the UNITY of His Believers, He was not praying for anyone or any who did not believe or should not believe on Him. Unity is only possible to those who believe on Jesus. Therefore, this prayer of our Lord cannot be made the basic for all the religious bodies regardless of what they believe. Jesus was praying for the Unity of those who should believe on Him. This does not embrace the Godless, Christ-denying, Christ-rejecting, unbelievers who may hold to some form of religion or those who have added to or taken away from the Holy Word of God. In Ephesians 4:1-6, there is a "Seven Fold" Unity. This seven fold is a complete Unity. The number seven denotes completeness as you will see further on in this book. When people possess the thing mentioned here and do what is mentioned there will be a complete Unity. Don't forget the fullness of number seven is the completeness, or perfection of God, or bringing a thing to an end.

Division or Separation
"TWO"

The number two is the Bible number for Division or Separation. When the body is divided into two parts there is a Division or Separation. It might be a peaceful Division, but usually it isn't.

In Genesis 10:25 it is stated, "And unto Eber were born two sons: the name of one was Peleg; for in his days was the earth divided;" Here the word "divided" is used in connection with number two. This passage was placed there for a purpose.

Luke 15:11 and 12, Jesus says, "A certain man had two sons: And the younger of them said to his father, Father, give me the portion of the goods that falleth to me. And he divided unto them his living." Here we find the number two connected with the word "divided." In the next verse, we find the younger son separating himself from his father and going into a far country. (Verse 13)

Now in John 10:18, the word "Power" is used twice and the next verse speaks of division, "No man taketh it from me, but I lay it down of myself, I have (1) power to lay it down, and I have (2) power to take it again. This commandment have I received of my Father." There was division among the Jews for this saying. (Verse 19) Again we find division connected with the number two.

Revelation 16:18 and 19, the word "divided" is again associated with the number two. "and there was a great (1) earthquake, such as was not since men were upon the earth, so mighty an (2) earthquake, and so great. And the great city was divided into three parts, and the cities of the nations fell: and great Babylon came in remembrance before God, to give unto her the cup of the wine of the fierceness of his wrath." In this place the word "Babylon" occurs the second time in the book of Revelation. The first time it occurs is in Revelation 14:8. By continuing on to Revelation 16:21 it will be

18

seen that the word "Hail" is used two times, and the word "Plague" is used two times. So in connection with the word "divided," the word "earthquake" occurs two times, the word "hail" is used two times, and the word "plague" is used two times, Babylon occurs the second time in the book of Revelation.

In Genesis 1:4 it's stated, "and God divided the light from the darkness." Here we find two things, "Light and Darkness" and the word "Divided" connected with them. In Genesis 1:14 God said, "Let there be lights in the firmament of the heaven to divide the day from the night;" Here are two things, day and night, and the word divided connected with them. Then in Genesis 1:16 is stated, "And God made two great lights; the greater light to rule the day, and the lesser light to rule the night:" There the two great lights divided the day and the night. In the days of Jereboam and Rehoboam the one nation of Israel divided into two kingdoms known as the house of Israel and the house of Judah. In Ezekiel 37:16-22, we find the Lord having Ezekiel to take two sticks and put them together and they should become one stick. Then the Lord said, "And say unto them, Thus saith the Lord God; Behold, I will take the children of Israel from among the heathen, whither they be gone, and will gather them on every side, and bring them into their own land: And I will make them one nation in the land upon the mountains of Israel; and one king shall be king to them all: and they shall be no more two nations, neither shall they be divided into two kingdoms any more at all:" See Ezekiel 37:21 and 22. The two nations show forth a divided condition. The two sticks pictured this division and when the two sticks became one in the hand of the prophet, the picture of the abolishment of that Division and a condition of Unity was brought again.

The same thing is seen in Hebrews 8:8-10. "For finding fault with them, he saith, Behold, the days come, saith the Lord, when I will make a new covenant with the house of (1) Israel and with the house of (2) Judah: Not according to the covenant that I made with their fathers in the day when I

19

took them by the hand to lead them out of the land of Egypt; because they continued not in my covenant, and I regarded them not, saith the Lord. For this is the covenant that I will make with the house of Israel after those days, saith the Lord; I will put my laws into their mind, and write them in their hearts: and I will be to them a God, and they shall be to me a people."

Now, dear reader, if you will observe that in the eighth verse there are two houses; that of (1) Israel and of (2) Judah. Here is set forth a divided condition of that people. On the other hand there is only one house in the tenth verse, and that is the house of Israel. The house of Judah has merged with the house of Israel, the division has been abolished by the work of the spirit in their heart, and now there is only one house, the house of Israel. This teaches the same lesson as Ezekiel's two sticks becoming one. They have become one nation, never to be divided again.

In I Kings 3:16-27, there is an account of two women contending over the ownership of two children, one dead and the other alive. They both have claimed the living child. Here are two women and two children and a division between the two women. The case was brought before Solomon to settle and as a test to find the true mother Solomon demanded the living child be divided and one half given to each of the women. The woman which caused the division asked that the living child be divided, but the woman who was the mother of the child asked that the child not to be killed but given to the other.

Number two is connected with division in Mark 6:41, "And when he had taken the five loaves and two fishes, he looked to heaven, and blessed, and brake the loaves, and gave them to his disciples to set before them; and the two fishes divided he among them all."

Acts 27:41 states, "And falling into a place where two seas met, they ran the ship aground; and the forepart stuck fast, and remained unmoveable, but the hinder part was broken with the violence of the waves." Here are two seas and a divided ship, the forepart sticking fast in the sand and the hinder part broken from the forepart and then there followed a divided opinion on what compensation to make of the prisoners. "And the soldiers' counsel was to kill the prisoners, lest any of them should swim out, and escape. But the centurion, willing to save Paul, kept them from their purpose;" So here we have two seas and a divided opinion.

There was a division in the church at Corinth. Read I Corinthians 1:1-11, I Corinthians 3:33 and I Corinthians 11:18. While pleading for Unity instead of Division Paul brings in the subject of baptism which he mentions six times. We find that six is Satan's number and he is the author of division in the churches. The second time Paul used the word "baptize" he mentions two whom he had baptized. He said, "I thank God that I baptized none of you, but (1) Crispus and (2) Gaius;" (I Corinthians 1:14). These were not all he had baptized for in the 16th verse he said he had also baptized the household of Stephanas. Two is the number for division and had Paul mentioned the household of Stephanas in the same connection with Crispus and Gaius, that would have been more than two. In the second place, Paul used the word "baptized" when he mentions two whom he had baptized, (1) Crispus and (2) Gaius.

In Acts 28:30 it is stated, "And Paul dwelt two whole years in his own hired house," When Paul would have set forth man's separation from sin he used the word "Baptized" two times. "What shall we say then? Shall we continue in sin that grace may abound? God Forbid. How shall we that are dead to sin live any longer therein? Know ye not that so many of us as were (1) baptized into Jesus Christ was (2) baptized into his death?" Death is a separation and baptism shows forth our separation.

In Acts 13:2, two names, the name of Barnabas and the name of Saul, are connected with the word "separate." "As they ministered to the Lord, and fasted, the Holy Ghost said, Separate me (1) Barnabas and (2) Saul for the work whereunto I have called them."

Resurrection
"THREE"

I'm going to bring you the number three which stands for Resurrection in the Bible next. I have known for years that the number three is associated with Resurrection. The evidence is so abundant that there is no excuse for Bible readers not to know this.

Jesus said to His critics, "Destroy this temple, and in three days I will raise it up." (John 2:19-21) "But he spoke of the temple of his body." (John 2:21)

Jesus said in Matthew 12:40, "For as Jonas was three days and three nights in the whale's belly; so shall the Son of man be three days and three nights in the heart of the earth." This verse tells us that our Lord was raised up from the dead after being dead three days and nights, and in this verse it talked about the number "three" four times. Four times three is 12. This is the Bible number for Divine Authority, Power or rule. It was the Divine power of God that brought forth Jesus from the dead. This is the way the number three is used four times in connection with our Lord's resurrection.

During Jesus' personal ministry He raised three from the dead. He raised the son of the widow of Nain (Luke 7:15); He raised the daughter of the ruler Jairus (Luke 8:41-55); and He raised Lazarus of Bethany. (John 11:43 & 44) When He called Lazarus forth from the grave He spoke three words, "Lazarus, come forth." These are also three words in the Greek language and the third one of these has just three letters. There were three members in the family of Lazarus: Mary, Martha and Lazarus. (John 11:1-3)

There are three records of the Sadducees asking Jesus about the resurrection of the seven men who had married the same woman. First, it is recorded in Matthew 22:23-32; secondly, in Mark 12:18-27; and, finally, in Luke 20:27-38. The book of John does not record the conversation. Thus the work of the Spirit can be seen in having three and only three records of this conversation. It was to show forth the number three as the number connected with the Resurrection.

In our Lord's reply to the Sadducees while speaking of the Resurrection, Jesus used the expression "the dead" three times. First in Luke 20:35; secondly, in Luke 20:37; and the final time in Luke 20:38. "Now, that the dead are raised, even Moses showed at the bush, when he called the Lord the (1) God of Abraham, and the (2) God of Isaac and the (3) God of Jacob. For he is not a God of the dead but of the living; for all live unto him." (Luke 20:37 & 38)

Three times Jesus said of those who came to Him and believed on Him, "I will raise him up at the last day." The first time He said this was in John 6:40, the second time in John 6:44 and the third time in John 6:54.

In the transfiguration scene when Moses and Elijah had appeared with Him and spoke of His death (Luke 9:28-31), He took with Him three of His disciples. If you will remember, it was Peter, James and John who were to be witnesses to this event. He said to the three disciples, "Tell the vision to no man, until the Son of man be risen again from the dead." (Matthew 17:9)

In connection with His trial and death, Jesus was denied by Peter three times. He was tried before three courts: Sanhedrin, Pilate and Herod. (Matthew 26:57-75, Matthew 27:1-25, Luke 23:4-11) He was crucified with two others making three crosses. (Matthew 27-38) There was an inscription placed on His cross and written in three languages which were Hebrew, Greek and Latin. (John 19:20) The sun was darkened for three hours. (Matthew 27:45)

Sons of God, the Holy Ghost must dwell in me in order to bring forth this record of the Bible to be something that should be inspiring to all who will read this book. The Bible records the names of three women who went to Jesus' grave the morning of His resurrection. They were Mary Magdalene, Mary the Mother of James and Salome. (Mark 16:1)

The third time Jesus manifested Himself to His disciples after His resurrection there was a miraculous draught of fish numbering 153. (John 21:2-14) The 14th verse shows that this was the third time Jesus showed Himself to His disciples after His resurrection. One hundred fifty-three divided by three equals 51 three times. Divide 51 by three again and the third manifestation will result in exactly 17, the number which I shall later show to be the number for Victory. Seventeen is the number for victory and the day of the month our Lord rose from the dead.

Now that we have some of the numerical proof shown in the New Testament, let us turn to the Old Testament and we'll see the same evidence.

There were three dead persons raised to life again in the Old Testament. The first instance was when Elisha raised the dead child of the widow of Zarephath. When Elisha raised the child he stretched his body three times over the child's body. (I Kings 17:21-22) The second was when Elisha raised the dead child of the Shunammite woman. (II Kings 4:16-36) When he raised him he put his mouth on the child's mouth, his eyes on the child's eyes and his hand on the child's hand. (Verses 34 & 35) Thirdly, a young man was restored to life when his body was let down into the grave of the prophet Elisha. (II Kings 13:21) In verse 18 of II Kings 13, you'll find a King striking the ground three times with an arrow. Why does the number three always appear when a resurrection has been performed? Surely it's the Lord's will!

There are three great titles for the Lord: Father, Son and Holy Ghost, and these three are one. Praise His Name for He is King of kings and Lord of lords!

Israel killed a Passover lamb, a type of Jesus. (I Corinthians 5:7) Three days after the Passover, they journeyed through the Red Sea where there is a figure of death and resurrection. (Exodus 8:7, 12:18-27, 14:1-31)

Hebrews 11:17-19 states that Abraham offered up his son and received him from the dead in a figure. They were three days journeying to the place of offering. (Genesis 22:1-4)

Aaron's rod which bore buds, blossoms and almonds is a figure of the resurrection. This is the order in which new life appears. The tree first puts forth a bud, then comes the bloom and then the fruit. The rod was the dead walking stick when Aaron brought it before the Lord. The next morning it had came to life and had buds, blossoms and almonds. (Numbers 17:8)

There are many other instances of resurrection in the Old Testament, but I believe that this will suffice to show that the Old and New Testaments compare. How could this be? The writers were living so far apart and couldn't have known each other, yet we know that the ALMIGHTY GOD was directing their hands and guiding their minds.

The first three times the name of Peter occurs in the book of Acts are found in Acts 1:13, 1:15 and 2:14. Acts 1:15 says that Peter "stood up" which is the Greek word for resurrection. When Peter's name is mentioned the third time in the book of Acts ("anastasis" means to stand up and three being the number for Resurrection), and where he stood up the second time he preached on the outpouring of the Holy Ghost which he said came as the result of the resurrection and ascension of Jesus. (Acts 2:14-37) In that particular sermon Peter said that Jesus was approved by (1) miracles and (2) wonders and (3) signs. (Verse 22) Peter quoted from David's prophecy about the resurrection of Jesus. (Verses 25-31) In this connection the name of David is used three times. (Verses 25, 29 & 34)

Acts 9:38, Peter's name occurs the 23rd time. (Twenty-three is the Bible number for Death which is later explained in this book.) Right before Peter's name occurs the 23rd time, Dorcas or Tabitha dies. (Verses 36 & 37) Peter's name occurs three more times and he raises her back to life again. (Verse 40) Amazing? It's just the beginning. Through the power of the Holy Ghost and the precious name of Jesus you're going to see that the Bible is the written Word of God. I only hope you'll want everyone to read this book for it was given by revelation.

Acts 17:1-3 states that Paul went into the Synagogues at Thessalonica for three Sabbath days and preached that Christ had to suffer in order to have risen again from the dead.

Acts 20:7-12 speaks of Paul raising a young man back to life who had fallen from the third loft. The third floor loft was inserted into the record to show that the number three is associated with the resurrection.

While speaking of the redemption of our bodies, Paul used the word "ourselves" three times. "not only they, but *ourselves* also, which have the firstfruits of the Spirit, even we *ourselves* groan within *ourselves*, waiting for the adoption, to wit, the redemption of our body." (Romans 8:23)

At the beginning of I Corinthians 15, Paul begins his great discourse on the subject of the resurrection. In the three previous chapters he had been writing about Spiritual gifts which were bestowed on us because of the resurrection. The whole chapter abounds in illustrations of how the number three is connected with the resurrection. The third time the word "and" occurs is where it is stated, "and that he arose again the third day." (I Corinthians 15:4) The word "Apostle" is found three times. (Verse 7 and two times in verse 9) Acts 1:22, 23, 4:33 and I Corinthians 9:1 show that the Apostles were eyewitnesses of the Lord's resurrection. In speaking of his apostleship Paul used the word "Grace" three times. In this connection the word "Heavenly" is found three times. I Corinthians 15:48 and 49 show the word "Adam" three times. In verse 22 it is stated, "In Adam all die —"; in verse 45, "the first man Adam was made a living soul; and the last Adam was made a quickening spirit." The third time the word "Adam" occurs gives reference to Jesus Christ, the quickening Spirit through Whom the resurrection comes. The word "Victory" is found three times. Victory is found in verses 54, 55 and 57. "Death" is found three times, verses 21, 26, and where it is stated, "So when this corruptible shall have put on incorruption and this mortal shall have put on immortality, then shall be brought to pass the saying that is written. Death is swallowed up in victory." (Verse 54)

Verses 22 and 24 set forth a threefold order in the resurrection, "For since by man came death, by man came also the resurrection of the dead. For as in Adam all die, even so in Christ shall all be made alive. But every man in his own order: Christ the firstfruits; afterward they that are Christ's at his coming. Then cometh the end, when he shall have delivered up the kingdom to God, even the Father; when he shall have put down all rule and all authority and power." (I Corinthians 15:21-24)

In verses 35-37 the word "Sow" is used three times in connection with the resurrection. "But some man will say, How are the dead raised up? and with what body do they come? Thou fool, that which thou sowest is not quickened, except it die: And that which thou sowest, thou sowest not that body that shall be, but bare grain, it may chance of wheat, or of some other grain:" So even nature itself bears testimony of the resurrection by numbers. Some time ago I saw a picture of a grain of wheat on a cereal box. Three parts of that grain were pointed out by arrows. The first part was the husk from which the bran comes, the second part was the main body from which flour comes and the third part was the germ from which the vitamin comes. It is this third part of the grain that quickens the sown wheat and produces the new plant. We know that Jesus is speaking of the necessity of His death and resurrection. He said, "Except a corn of wheat fall into the ground and die, it abideth alone: but if it dies, it bringeth forth much fruit." (John 12:24) So the three parts to the grain of wheat are sown; the third part of which quickens and brings forth new life which is nature's testimony to the resurrection. The number of the resurrection is three. The three parts of the grain of wheat, the third part bringing forth new life, is in keeping with the testimony of the scriptures.

The resurrection is further demonstrated by three heavenly bodies: "There is one glory of the *sun*, and another glory of the *moon*, and another glory of the *stars*: for one star differeth from another star in glory. SO ALSO IS THE RESURRECTION of the dead. It is sown in corruption; it is raised in incorruption:" (I Corinthians 15:41 & 42) The sun races across the sky to set out of sight, but it doesn't stay down, it rises again. So man comes upon the scene to pass across the stage of life, and as the sun he goes down to be seen no more until he rises again. The moon comes up to pass across the heavens and then out of sight, as do the stars. The next night they rise again. So it is with man. When God set those heavenly bodies in their places, He said, "let them be for signs, for seasons, for days, and years:" (Genesis 1:14) When Jesus was born the stars gave a sign. (Matthew 2:1 & 2) When Jesus was on the cross the sun was darkened for three hours. "Now from the sixth hour there was darkness over all the land unto the ninth hour." (Matthew 27:45) After the sun was hid for three hours it appeared again. So Jesus went into the darkness of death for three days, and after three days He rose again. The sun, moon and stars will witness to the return of Jesus. Jesus said, "And there shall be signs in the *sun*, and in the *moon* and in the *stars*." (Luke 21:25)

When the new heaven and the new earth shall come, there will be no more death. "And there shall be no more death," (Revelation 21:4) When there is no more death there will be no need of these heavenly bodies to witness concerning the resurrection. Revelation 21:23 states, "And the city had no need of the sun, neither of the moon, to shine in it: for the glory of God did lighten it, and the Lamb is the light thereof." Then Revelation 21:4 states, "and there shall be no more death," When it is stated that death shall be no more, there is no need of the sun and moon, thus there is no need for death or resurrection.

Everything in the Bible and nature testifies to the glorious truth of the Blessed Resurrection. We may go down to the darkness of death and the grave but just as surely as Jesus rose again we shall rise. Just as truly, the grain of wheat quickening into new life is proof that we will rise again. Just as certain as the sun is to rise on the morrow, we are certain to rise on God's golden tomorrow. The overwhelming testimony of the Bible numbers along with the many positive statements from God's word makes our hope sure and stedfast.

When I received this revelation of Jesus Christ I became sound in God's Word. I became so sound I didn't want to break even the infinity of this precious Word. Since our hope is sure and stedfast, Paul closes that wonderful chapter on the resurrection with a threefold admonishment, "Therefore, my beloved brethren, be ye *stedfast, unmovable*, always *abounding* in the work of the Lord forasmuch as ye know that your labour is not in vain in the Lord." (I Corinthians 15:58)

I could go on and on until I fully convince everyone who reads this book on this glorious revelation that Jesus gave me. If I did, it would fill hundreds of volumes. As the Lord directs and inspires my mind, heart and soul, I shall bring it forth. I Thessalonians 4:16 and 17 states, "For the Lord himself shall descend from heaven with a *shout*, and with the *voice* of the Archangel, and with the *trump* of God: and the dead in Christ shall rise first: Then we which are alive and remain shall be caught up together with them in the clouds, to meet the Lord in the air: and so shall we EVER BE WITH THE LORD." What a glorious meeting that will be!!!

Our Lord's closing testimony will be from the last book of the Holy Bible. "And when I saw him, I fell at his feet as dead. And he laid his right hand upon me, saying unto me, FEAR not; I am the first and the last: I am he that *liveth*, and was *dead*; and, behold I am *alive for evermore*, Amen; and have the keys of hell and of death." (Revelation 1:17 & 18) There are three things said about our Lord's life, death and resurrection. "I am alive for evermore." Then follows the word "Amen." This is the third time "Amen" occurs in the book of Revelation. Note verses 6 and 7, the third time followed with the expression that sets forth His resurrection. "I am alive for evermore,"

Jesus starts with the words, "Fear not," and none can banish fear as He can. None can give courage in the face of death like Jesus. The time will come for God's children to go through the valley of death and the great Shepherd will be there to lead His sheep safely through to the shining portals of glory beyond. When the Hebrew children were called upon to pass through the fiery furnace, which was as a picture of death, there was another party there. Praise God! That other party was said to be "like the Son of God." The Hebrew children had expressed their faith in God's power Who did deliver them. (Daniel 3:17) He was with them when they had to go into the burning jaws of death. Picture that fiery furnace! It had no power to burn them because of God's presence. They came out alive without a hair being singed, without their coats changed or the smell of fire upon them. (Verse 27) The furnace of death couldn't and didn't leave its mark upon them. The Hebrew children passing through this furnace is a picture of the children of God going through death and resurrection. We need not fear death! He Who said unto John, "fear not", will be with you in that hour and will bring you safely through as He did the Hebrew children. Like them, we will come out without a trace of death or sickness, without affliction, aching heads, sightless eyes; death will be no more. God has the keys to hell and death and will bring us out of the furnace of death to suffer no more, to be with Him Who is the "Resurrection and the Life."

The First Creation
"FOUR"

The number four is associated with the First Creation and the Flesh. When applied to man it represents the Flesh in an unsaved state. This is true with one exception, Jesus Christ, Who was made Flesh but not in a sinful state. The fourth time Jesus is called the "Word" is in John 1:14, "And the Word was made flesh, and dwelt among us," The word "Amen" is found the fourth time in Revelation 3:14; Jesus is speaking to the Church at Laodicean, saying, "These things saith the Amen, the faithful and true witness, the beginning of the creation of God;" The word "Amen" occurred in Revelation 1:6, 1:7 and 1:18, which you'll notice was used in connection with number three or the resurrection.

I Corinthians 15:39, Paul speaks of the word "flesh", and it's used four times. "All flesh is not the same flesh: but there is one kind of flesh of *men*, another flesh of *beasts*, another of *fishes*, and another of *birds*." The reader's attention is called to the way the numerology is preserved in this verse. The word "Flesh" occurs twice before Paul lists the four kinds of flesh, and then it is only used two more times, which makes four times in all. While speaking of men and beasts, he said, "There is one kind of Flesh of Men, another flesh of beasts," but in speaking of the flesh of birds and fishes the word is dropped, and he simply says, "another of fishes and another of birds." Speaking of the four different kinds of flesh, you'll notice that flesh is used four times although it was used twice already. Note the way the numerology of the passage is used and how it corresponds with the number which means Creation and Flesh. The word "Creature" is found four times in the account of Creation. (Genesis 1:20, 1:21, 1:24 & 2:19) The verb "Created" is found seven times, and later it will be seen where this fits in.

The first four Bible numbers are found in the opening statement, "In the beginning God created the heaven and the earth." (Genesis 1:1) John 1:1 shows that the "Word", WHICH is Jesus, was with God in the beginning. Genesis 1:2 shows that the Spirit was there; and the opening verse also shows the God-head and the Unity of the God-head. In this verse Creation is found which is the number four. Then there are two things mentioned that were created: the heaven and the earth. Number two stands for Division. Division is connected with the heaven and earth. (Verses 6-8) The word "beginning" is a noun used as a commencement of an action or state. So there are four nouns in the opening statement of God's work of Creation: the *beginning, God, heaven* and *earth.*

Four things are said about the lights which God created: "And God said, Let there be lights in the firmament of the heaven to divide the day from the night; and let them be for *signs*, and for *seasons*, and for *days*, and *years*:" (Genesis 1:14) There are four seasons in the year which are: spring, summer, autumn and winter. There are four tides in a day and night: two incoming and two outcoming.

The river that flowed out of the Garden of Eden was parted in to four heads. "River" occurs four times in Genesis 2:10-14, "And a (1) river went out of Eden to water the garden; and from thence it was parted, and became into four heads. The name of the first is Pison: that is it which compasseth the whole land of Havilah, where there is gold; And the gold of that land is good: there is bdellium and the onyx stone. And the name of the second (2) river is Gihon: the same is it that compasseth the whole land of Ethiopia. And the name of the third (3) river is Hiddekel: that is it which goeth toward the east of Assyria. And the fourth (4) river is Euphrates." Here the numerology of the passage is safely guarded to show creation. The word "River" is mentioned one time before each name of the four "Rivers", yet the word "River" occurs only four times in the whole passage. This is done by omitting the word "River" in naming the first one and is simply stated, "The name of the first is Pison:"

When God was going to send the flood, He mentioned four things in connection with what He had created, "And the Lord said, I will destroy man whom I have created from the face of the earth, both *man*, *beast*, the *creeping things* and the *fowls of the air*." (Genesis 6:7) This occurred again in Genesis 7:23, where the word "Cattle" is used instead of "Beast", "And every living substances was destroyed which was upon the face of the ground, both *man*, and *cattle*, and the *creeping things*, and the *fowl of the heaven*;"

In Ezekiel 1:5-17, Elisha had a vision in which he saw four living creatures. The four living creatures had four faces, four wings, and four sides. Here the number four is repeated four times. There are four living creatures, then there are four faces, four wings, and four sides. Amazing? It only shows God's word to be perfect. Romans 1:23 states that man "changed the glory of the uncorruptible God into an image made like to *corruptible man*, and to *birds*, and *four-footed beasts*, and *creeping things*." Then he goes on to say that they "changed the truth of God into a lie, and worshipped and served the creature more than the Creator," Romans 1:25 lists the four things that were just mentioned to prove that the number four is connected with creation. "Thou carryest them away as with a flood; they are as asleep: in the morning they are like grass which groweth up. In the morning it *flourisheth*, and *groweth up*; in the evening it is cut down, and withereth." (Psalm 90:5 and 6 speaks of man.)

Isaiah 40:4-8 shows the word "Grass" and it's used four times, "All flesh is *grass* and all the goodliness thereof is as the flower of the field: The *grass* withereth, the flower fadeth: because the Spirit of the Lord bloweth upon it: surely the people is *grass*. The grass withereth, the flower fadeth: but the word of our God shall stand for ever." (Verses 6-8 show grass mentioned four times.)

In Romans 8:19-22, the word "Creature" occurs three times and the creation once which makes four. Both of the translations as rendered, "For the earnest expectation of the *creature* waiteth for the manifestation of the sons of God. For the *creature* was made subject to vanity, not willingly, but by reason of him who hath subjected the same in hope. Because the creature itself also shall be delivered from the bondage of corruption into the glorious liberty of the children of God. For we know that the whole *creation* groaneth and travaileth in pain together until now." The old American revised translation renders the word "Creation" in all four places; the Greek word is the same also.

When it says that "all of the creation groaneth and travails together," it teaches that all of God's Kingdom is awaiting the unifying of all into one. The earth was cursed with thorns and thistles because of man's sin, and the animal creation was cursed as well. (Genesis 3:14-18) The time is coming when this bondage shall be lifted from creation. Instead of thorns shall come up the fir tree, and instead of the brier shall come up the myrtle tree. (Isaiah 55:13) "The wolf also shall dwell with the lamb, and the leopard shall lie down with the kid; and the calf and the young lion and the fatling together; and a little child shall lead them, And the cow and the bear shall feed; their young ones shall lie down together: and the lion shall eat straw like the ox." (Isaiah 11:6 & 7) Before the fall, all animals ate green herbs. (Genesis 1:30) The above Prophecy will be as literally fulfilled as were the passages in Genesis 1:30, which refers to all of the animals eating the green herbs.

Colossians 1:16 states that there are four things which God created, "For by him were all things created, that are in heaven, and that are in earth, visible and invisible, whether they be *thrones*, or *dominions*, or *principalities*, or *powers*:"

Revelation 5:13 shows the creatures in four different places giving praise to the Father and the Son in four words, "And every creature which is (1) in heaven, and on (2) the earth, and (3) under the earth, and such as are (4) in the sea, and all that are in them, heard I saying, (1) Blessing, and (2) honour, and (3) glory, and (4) power, be unto him that sitteth upon the throne, and unto the Lamb for ever and ever." Why are the creatures mentioned in only four places? It was to show that four is the number associated with creation! In Mark 16:15, it is found that Jesus sent out His disciples to preach the gospel to every creature. In Acts 1:8, He said, "ye shall be witnesses unto me both in *Jerusalem*, and in all *Judaea*, and in *Samaria*, and unto the *uttermost part of the earth*." He couldn't have mentioned Galilee, Syria, Italy or other places by name because four is the number of creation.

Peter had to have a special vision given him showing that the gospel was for every creature. In that vision he saw a blanket let down from heaven like a sheet knit at the four corners. In this vessel he saw a *four-footed beast*, and *creeping things* and *wild beast* and *fowls of the air*. (Acts 10:1-12) This convinced Peter that the gospel was "to every *nation*, and *kindred*, and *tongue*, and *people*," (Revelation 14:6) When Peter reached the home of Cornelius it had been exactly four days to the hour since the Angel of the Lord had told Cornelius to send for Peter. (Acts 10:30)

The word "ungodly" is connected four times with the wicked in Jude 14 and 15, "And Enoch also, the seventh from Adam prophesied of these, saying, Behold the Lord cometh with ten thousand of his saints, To execute judgment upon all, and to convince all that are *ungodly* among them of all their *ungodly* deeds which they have *ungodly* committed, and of all their hard speeches which *ungodly* sinners have spoken against him."

Ishmael, the son of Abraham by the bondswoman, was said to be born after the flesh. (Galatians 4:22, 23) Four things were foretold to Ishmael, "the Lord said to her, Behold, thou art with child, and shall bear a son and shall call his name Ishmael; because the Lord hath heard thy affliction. And he will be (1) a wild man; (2) his hand will be against every man, and (3) every man's hand against him; and he shall (4) dwell in the presence of all his brethren." (Genesis 16:11-12)

All of these things show forth that the number four is connected with the first creation and the natural or unsaved man.

In I Corinthians 1:26-28, Paul stated, "how that not many wise men after the flesh, not many mighty, not many noble, are called:" Then he stated that the purpose of this was, "That no flesh should glory in his presence." (Verse 29) He went on to say, "But of him are ye in Christ Jesus, who of God is made unto us *wisdom*, and *righteousness*, and *sanctification*, and *redemption*: That according as it is written, He that glorieth, let him glory in the Lord." (Verse 30) These particular four things were mentioned at this time because man shouldn't glory in the flesh and flesh is represented by the number four.

In Luke 17:26 and 27, Jesus said, "And as it was in the days of Noe, so shall it be also in the days of the Son of Man. They did *eat*, they *drank*, they *married wives*, they *were giving in marriage*, until the day that Noe entered into the ark, and the flood came, and destroyed them all." These were four things man was doing in the days of Noah. Genesis 6:12 shows, "And God looked upon the earth, and behold, it was corrupt; for all flesh had corrupted his way upon the earth."

Grace
"FIVE"

The natural man, represented by four and in a lost state, stands in need of Grace. So the next number, Five, stands for Grace. When God created man He had in mind a manifestation of His Grace, "Who hath saved us, and called us with an holy calling, not according to our works, but according to his own purpose and grace, which was given us in Christ Jesus before the world began," (II Timothy 1:9)

The word "Grace" occurs five times in Romans 11:5 and 6, while the word "Work" is found only four times. Paul said, "Even so then at this present time also there is a remnant according to the election of *Grace*. And if by *grace*, then is it no more of works: otherwise *grace* is no more *grace*. But if it be of works, then is it no more *grace*: otherwise work is no more work."

The natural man, who is represented by the number four, depends upon his works for salvation. The Children of God depend upon grace, which is represented by the number five. The word "grace" also occurs five times in Exodus 33:12-17. This took place in a conversation between God and Moses just after Israel had sinned in making the golden calf. You'll find in Exodus 32:1-35 that Israel had said, "All that the Lord hath spoken we will do." But they had failed to do what God had commanded and they broke God's law. (Exodus 19:8) They had become guilty sinners before God and condemned before the law that they had failed to keep. It was at such a time that God's grace, which is the one and only hope for mankind, came into the picture. It was not until Paul had proven there was no justification by the Law and that the Law pronounced the whole world guilty before God that he came to the glorious truth of men being justified, freed by God's grace. (Romans 3:9-24) In the 32nd and 33rd chapters of Exodus, grace was revealed after the Law had been broken, and here the word "Grace" appears five times in our Lord's conversation with Moses, Israel's intercessor at that time. It is found first in Exodus 33:12, the second and third times in Exodus 33:13, the fourth in Exodus 33:16, and the fifth in Exodus 33:17. Five things are connected with grace. In Genesis 32:5, Jacob said to Esau, "And I have *Oxen*, and *asses, flocks*, and *manservants* and *womenservants*: and I have sent to tell my lord, that I may find grace in thy sight."

The fifth time the name of Noah appears is where it is said that, "Noah found grace in the eyes of the Lord." (Genesis 6:8)

The name of Ruth is found the fifth time in Ruth 2:2, "And Ruth the Moabitess said unto Naomi, Let me now go to the field, and glean ears of corn after him whose sight I shall find grace. And she said unto her, Go, my daughter."

The name of Boaz occurs the fifth time where they told Ruth to abide fast by her maidens until the end of the harvest, "Then she fell on her face, and bowed herself to the ground, and said unto him, Why have I found grace in thine eyes, that thou shouldest take knowledge of me, seeing I am a stranger?" (See Ruth 2:8-10.)

The fifth time the name of David is found is in I Samuel 16:22, where Saul sent to Jesse and said, "Let David, I pray thee, stand before me; for he hath found favour in my sight." The fifth time the word "God" is found in the book of Ephesians it is connected with "Grace." (Ephesians 2:4 & 5) The fifth time the word "Grace" occurs is in Ephesians 2:8, "For by grace are ye saved through faith; and that not of yourselves: it is the gift of God:"

The words "much more" which are connected with

37

"Grace" are found in Romans 5:9, 5:10, 5:15, 5:17 and 5:20. How fitting it is that these words are found the fifth time where it is said, "But where sin abounded, grace did much more abound:" (Romans 5:20)

II Corinthians 8:7 shows five things preceding the word "Grace", "Therefore, as ye abound in every thing, in *faith*, and *utterance*, and *knowledge*, and in *all diligence*, and in your *love* to us, see that ye abound in this grace also." Paul prayed to the Lord three times for the thorn to depart out of his flesh. God said to him, "My grace is sufficient for thee:" In this statement there are five Greek words. Because of what the Lord said, Paul went on to say, "Therefore I take pleasure in *infirmities*, in *reproaches*, in *necessities*, in *persecutions*, in *distresses*, for Christ's sake: for when I am weak, then am I strong." (II Corinthians 12:7-10)

Paul prayed three times for the Lord to take away the thorn from his flesh. The Lord gave grace instead and permitted the thorn to remain while Paul was in the flesh. When Paul comes out of the grace at the resurrection, which is represented by the number three and by the three times that he prayed concerning this thing, then the thorn will have been removed. How Beautiful! The number five is a divine pattern in God's order of things.

John 1:17 states, "grace and truth came by Jesus Christ." Isaiah mentioned five things Christ would be called, "his name shall be called (1) Wonderful, (2) Counsellor, (3) The mighty God, (4) The everlasting Father, (5) The Prince of Peace." (Isaiah 9:6)

Jesus descended from Noah through Shem. (Genesis 11:10-26, Luke 3:23-36) Shem had five sons, "the children of Shem are Elam, Asshur, Arphaxad, Lud and Aram." The name of Arphaxad is the third in the list and Jesus came through the line of Arphaxad. So in this verse, there is pictured the grace and the resurrection that is in Jesus.

It is evident that our Lord sprang out of the tribe of Judah. (Hebrews 7:14) Judah also had five sons, "And the sons of Judah; Er, and Onan, and Shelah, and Pharez and Zerah:

but Er and Onan died in the land of Canaan." (Genesis 46:12) Neither Er nor Onan left any children. This left only three to carry the seed of Judah. In the five sons this is the number for grace. The two that died show death and separation as seen; the number two which is separation or division. In the three that were left you'll see it stands for resurrection. All of these things are connected with the work of Jesus Who came from the tribe of Judah.

The infinite wisdom and power of God shows in His numbering system which was designed before the dawn of creation. The wisdom and foreknowledge of God enabled Him to fit in the lives, deeds and experiences of Bible characters to show forth God's work in the ages which are to come. You can't compare the mind of man with God's wisdom and power! It's no wonder Paul exclaimed, "O the depth of riches both of the wisdom and knowledge of God!" (Romans 11:33) Where in all the writings of man can anything be found that will begin to compare with this? Men try to destroy the numbering system in the King James Version of the Bible, but we know that it was brought forth by the hand of God.

In Romans 4:13-16, Paul states the promise to Abraham and his seed that they should be heirs of the world; he didn't mean through the law, but through the righteousness which is by faith. He went on to say, "Therefore it is of faith that it might be by Grace;" This is aligned with Genesis 15:6 and 9, "And he believed in the Lord; and he counted it to him for righteousness." "And he said unto him, Take me (1) an heifer of three years old, and (2) a she goat of three years old, and (3) a ram of three years old, and (4) a turtledove and (5) a young pigeon." These five offerings signify the grace through which Abraham and his seed are heirs of God. The three offerings that are connected with the three years signify this will be after Abraham has risen from the dead.

Bible? Absolutely! In Genesis 15:18, we read, "In the same day the Lord made a covenant with Abram, saying, Unto thy seed have I given this land, from the *river* of Egypt into the great *river*, the *river* Euphrates:" Notice the word "river" is found three times. Three is the number for the resurrection, and is still further proof that the resurrection of the saved must take place before the seed of Abraham enters into the possession of Canaan, under the Abrahamic covenant. In this place the name of Abram occurs the 42nd time. The number 42 is connected with the coming of Jesus. The third beatitude is, "Blessed are the meek: for they shall inherit the earth." (Matthew 5:5) This again connects the inheritance of the earth by the saints with the resurrection number three.

In Numbers 3:46-48, number five is found connected with redemption, "And for those that are to be redeemed of the two hundred and threescore and thirteen of the firstborn of the children of Israel, which are more than the Levites; Thou shalt even take five shekels apiece by the poll," "In whom we have redemption through his blood, the forgiveness of sins, according to the riches of his Grace;" (Ephesians 1:7) The five shekels of money paid pictured the richness of God's grace according to which we are redeemed.

When David went out in faith to meet the giant, he took five smooth stones out of the brook. (I Samuel 17:40) This represents the grace through which a child of God overcomes the world. In Romans 8:28-30, we find (1) Foreknowledge, (2) Predestination, (3) Calling, (4) Justification, and (5) Glorification connected with God's purpose concerning His people. This is grace reaching from before the world and into the glorification of the children of God in the age to come which was designed and worked out in the mind of God before the world.

The brazen altar in the Court of the Tabernacle was five cubits long, five cubits wide, and it had five vessels connected with it. (Exodus 27:1-3) The court which was five cubits high, "The length of the court shall be a hundred cubits, and the breadth fifty every where, and the height five cubits of fine twined linen." (Exodus 27:18) Grace shuts in the believers on every side.

Hebrews 2:9 shows us the picture of the cross of Jesus, "that he by the grace of God should taste death for every man." The four horns to which the sacrifice was tied (Psalm 22:16) represented the four places where the two hands and the two feet of Jesus were fastened to the tree. The Psalmist said of Him, "they pierced my hands and my feet." (Psalm 22:16) The number five connected with the altar represents the grace which His death on the tree brought to us.

In Galatians 4:22 and 23, it is stated, "the one by a bondmaid, the other by a freewoman. But he who was of the bondwoman was born after the flesh; but he of the freewoman was by promise." Then in Galatians 4:28, we read, "Now we, brethren, as Isaac was, are the children of promise." And Ishmael, the bondwoman's son, was circumcised when 13 years old. (Genesis 17:25) In Genesis 21:4, we find that Isaac was circumcised when eight days old. Now the difference between the one after the flesh and the child of promise is one under the law and one under grace. As more of the numbers are shown, the picture will become more interesting and enlightening.

Satan — His Influence
"SIX"

Six is the number connected with Satan, the Devil; his influence on man and his evil deeds and false worship.

"Against" is found six times in connection with the believers' warfare with the devil. "Put on the whole armour of God, that ye may be able to stand *against* the wiles of the devil, For we wrestle not *against* flesh and blood, but *against* principalities, *against* powers, *against* the rulers of the darkness of this world, *against* spiritual wickedness in high places." (Ephesians 6:11 & 12)

In Matthew's account of the temptation, the word "Devil"

is found four times, the word "Satan" once and the word "Tempter" once, making six times that the devil is referenced. (Matthew 4:1-13)

The sixth time Job's name occurs, in Job 1:9, it is connected with Satan. "Then Satan answered the Lord, and said, Doth Job fear God for nought?"

The sixth commandment was "thou shalt not kill." (Exodus 20:13) "Ye are of your father the devil, and the lusts of your father ye will do. He was a murderer from the beginning," (John 8:44) The sixth commandment was against murder. Jesus called the devil a murderer from the beginning. The statement, "Ye are of your father the devil," is six Greek words.

When Israel made the golden calf they did six things: "(1) they rose up early on the morrow, (2) and offered burnt offerings, (3) and brought peace offerings; (4) and the people sat down to eat (5) and to drink, and (6) rose up to play." (Exodus 32:6)

The children of Israel lusted after six things in the wilderness, "And the mixed multitudes that was among them fell a lusting: and the children of Israel also wept again, and said, Who shall give us flesh to eat? We remember the *fish*, which we did eat in Egypt freely; the *cucumbers*, and the *melons*, and the *leeks*, and the *onions* and the *garlick*." (Numbers 11:4 & 5) When Haman's name occurs the sixth time in Esther 3:6, he plans to kill all the Jews. The hand of the devil tried to destroy God's chosen people, the nation through which Jesus was to come. The 12 years of Omri's reign was divided into two periods of six years each. He reigned six years in Tirzah and six years in Samares, and then it is stated, "But Omir wrought evil in the eyes of the Lord, and did worse than all that were before him." (I Kings 16:22-25)

The image of Nebuchadnezzar (Daniel 3:1-5) set up to be worshipped was six cubits broad and they played six kinds of musical instruments when the people were called upon to worship the image. Balshazzar and his lords praised the gods of *gold, silver, brass, iron, wood* and *stone*. (Daniel 5:4)

42

In I Corinthians 5:1-5, Paul told the church at Corinth to deliver over to Satan the fornicator who had his father's wife. In I Corinthians 5:11, he lists six kinds of men with whom they were not to eat. "But now I have written unto you not to keep company, if any man that is called a brother be a *fornicator*, or *covetous*, or *idolater*, or a *railer*, or a *drunkard*, or an *extortioner*; with such an one no not to eat."

Ephesians 2:1 and 2 states, "And you hath he quickened, who were dead in trespasses and sins; Wherein in time past ye walked according to the course of this world, according to the prince of the power of the air, the spirit that now worketh in the children of disobedience:" Peter mentioned six things which the believer had done in time past, "For the time past of our life may suffice us to have wrought the will of the Gentiles, when we walked in *lasciviousness, lusts, excess of wine, revellings, banquetings*, and *abominable idolatries*:" (I Peter 4:3)

At the sounding of the sixth trumpet, men are found worshipping six false gods, "And the rest of the men which were not killed by these plagues yet repented not of the works of their hands, that they should not worship *devils*, and *idols of gold*, and *silver*, and *brass*, and *stone*, and of *wood*: which neither can see, nor hear, nor walk:" (Revelation 9:13-20) In Revelation, John is shown the judgment of the great whore which setteth upon many water. This whore is called a woman six times in chapter 17:3, 17:4, 17:6, 17:7, 17:9 and 17:18. She is said to be "that great city, which reigneth over the kings of the earth." "And upon her forehead was a name written, MYSTERY BABYLON THE GREAT THE MOTHER OF HARLOTS AND ABOMINATIONS OF THE EARTH." The word "Babylon" is found six times in the book of Revelation (14:8, 16:19, 17:5, 18:2, 18:10 and the sixth time in 18:21). This woman is said to be adorned in six things, "And the woman was arrayed in *purple* and *scarlet* colour, and decked with *gold* and *precious stones*, and *pearls*, having a *golden cup* in her hand full of abominations and filthiness of her fornication:" (Revelation 17:4) Revelation

18:16 is where she is called a city. Six things are said about her, "And saying, Alas, alas, that great city, that was clothed in (1) fine linen, and (2) purple, and (3) scarlet, and decked with (4) gold, and (5) precious stones, and (6) pearls!" The sixth time the one thousand years is mentioned in Revelation 20:1-7, it is connected with Satan. "And when the thousand years are expired, Satan shall be loosed out of his prison,"

In many places six Greek words are used in connection with the devil. "And one of you is a devil?" (John 6:70) "Ye are of your father the devil," (John 8:44) "These are not the words of him that hath a devil." (John 10:21) "Can a devil open the eyes of the blind?" (John 10:21) "the devils also believe, and tremble." (James 2:19)

In Luke 5:21, the scribes and Pharisees accuse Jesus of blaspheming, and they ask, "Who is this which speaketh blasphemies?" This has six Greek words and also six English words. Pilate asked the chief priests, "Shall I crucify your King?" And they answered by saying, "We have no king but Caesar." (John 19:15)

In the works of the flesh as given in Galatians 5:19-21, the sixth one is "witchcraft." Paul called Elmis, the sorcerer, "A child of the devil." The book of Galatians was written for the purpose of counteracting the evil influence of false teachers who were trying to bring the Galatians under bondage of the law again. The word "bondage" is found six times in that book. They are in chapters 2:4, 4:3, 4:9, 4:24, 4:25 and 5:1.

Some time ago I was asked how to connect the six things in I Timothy 3:16 with the devil. The divisions in the verses are as follows, "And without controversy great is the mystery of godliness: GOD WAS MANIFEST IN THE FLESH, JUSTI-FIED IN THE SPIRIT, SEEN OF ANGELS, PREACHED UPON TO THE GENTILES, BELIEVED ON IN THE WORLD, RECEIVED UP INTO GLORY." The first of the statements is, "God was manifest in the Flesh." John said, "For this purpose the Son of God was manifested, that he might destroy the works of the devil." (I John 3:8) The second statement is "Justified in the Spirit". Immediately

44

following the descent of the Spirit upon Jesus, He was led up by the Spirit into the wilderness to be tempted of the devil. (Matthew 3:17-4:11) The third statement, "seen of Angels," stands for resurrection. The devil made Judas betray Jesus into the hands of the chief priest who put Him to death. God raised Him from the dead on the morning of the resurrection. The angels were at the tomb to witness His resurrection. (Luke 24:1-6) The devil set about to cover up the evidence of His resurrection by having the guards bribed to tell that while they slept the disciples came and stole Him away. (Matthew 28:11-15) If His body was stolen away while they were asleep, how did they know who stole Him? The fourth statement is "preached unto the Gentiles," "For ye, brethren, became followers of the churches of God which in Judaea are in Christ Jesus: for ye also have suffered like things of your own countrymen, even as they have of the Jews: Who both killed the Lord Jesus, and their own prophets, and have persecuted us; and they please not God, and are contrary to all men: Forbidding us to speak to the Gentiles that they might be saved, to fill up their sins alway: for the wrath is come upon them to the uttermost." (I Thessalonians 2:14-16) The fifth statement is, "believed on in the world," The devil tries to keep people from believing on Jesus, "But if our gospel be hid, it is hid to them that are lost: In whom the god of this world hath blinded the minds of them which believe not, lest the light of the glorious gospel of Christ, who is the image of God, should shine unto them." (II Corinthians 4:3-4) The sixth statement is, "Received up into Glory," Jesus' ascension to heaven was manifested by His triumph over all principalities, powers and dominions. (Ephesians 1:19-21, 6:11, 7:12)

In Luke 17:28, Jesus mentioned six things in connection with the wicked in Lot's time. "Likewise also as it was in the days of Lot; they did *eat*, they *drank*, they *bought*, they *sold*, they *planted*, they *builded*; But the same day that Lot went out of Sodom it rained fire and brimstone from heaven, and destroyed them all."

Revelation 13:2 states that the dragon, who is the devil, will give to the beast his power. There are 36 references to the beast in the book of Revelation. When added together, one to 36 total 666. Revelation 13:5 states that power is given to the beast to continue 42 months. Six, the number of Satan, added to 36, the number of times the beast is mentioned, equals 42, which is the exact number of months the beast will continue. In the face of such evidence who can deny that six is the number connected with Satan's influence?

Completeness, Perfection or Bringing to an End "SEVEN"

Number seven is connected with completeness, perfection, or bringing to an end. You're in a host of sevens now! Completeness, seven, for years has been considered by many Bible students as signifying completeness. The strange thing is that so many have never thought the other numbers have significance also.

In the beginning, God stamped number seven as the number connected with the finishing, completing or ending. "Thus the heavens and the earth were finished, and all the hosts of them. And on the seventh day God ended his work which he had made;" (Genesis 2:1 & 2)

God appointed seven days to the week. Everyone considers seven days as being a week. Our everyday life is regulated accordingly, but no one asks why! There are seven notes in the musical scale: A B C D E F G or DO RE MI FA SO LA TI. Man named the notes even as he did the days of the week, but he did not arrange the sound any more than he selected the number of days in a week. This was God's work as predestined.

In Leviticus 23:15, the word "complete" is found with the number seven. "And ye shall count unto you from the morrow after the sabbath, from the day that ye brought the sheaf of the wave offering; seven sabbaths shall be complete:" In Revelation 10:7, the word "finish" is found with the number seven, "But in the days of the voice of the seventh angel, when he shall begin to sound, the mystery of God should be finished, as he hath declared to his servants the prophets."

Revelation 16:17 states, "It is done." "And the seventh angel poured out his vial into the air; and there came a great voice out of the temple of heaven, from the throne, saying, It is done." There are exactly seven Greek letters in the verb, "It is done." Revelation 16:17 has just seven Greek letters in each word. In this connection the seventh angel poured out the seventh vial. Seven vials multiplied by seven angels would be 49; seven words multiplied by seven letters would be 49. In Revelation 16:17. it is seen that the judgment of the seven vials came upon the followers of the beast and dragon. The beast is mentioned 36 times in Revelation, and the word "dragon" is found 13 times. These two numbers combine to 49. The Greek word for "it is done" is GEGNON. Revelation 15:6 and 7 states, "And the seven angels came out of the temple, having the seven plagues, clothed in pure and white linen, and having their breasts girded with golden girdles. And one of the four beasts gave unto the seven angels seven golden vials full of the wrath of God, who liveth for ever and ever." In this verse there are 49 Greek words. This is seven times seven and there are seven angels with seven vials. The name of Noah occurs the seventh time where it is said, "Noah was a just man and perfect in his generation," (Genesis 6:9)

There are seven Greek words in the statement, "for my strength is made perfect in weakness." (II Corinthians 12:9)

It was seven days after Noah and his family entered the ark before the flood came. "And it came to pass after seven days, that the waters of the flood were upon the earth." (Genesis 7:10) In verse 10 the word "earth" is found the 49th time. The flood was indicative of God's wrath being poured out upon the earth even as the seven vials of the seven angels are to be connected with the wrath of God on the earth. "And I heard a great voice out of the temple saying to the seven angels, Go your ways, and pour out the vials of the wrath of God upon the earth." (Revelation 16:1) When seven, the number of angels, is multiplied by seven, the number of vials, the sum is 49. When the word "earth" is found the 49th time, God caused the flood to cover the earth. God had already said, "yet seven days, and I will cause it to rain upon the earth forty days and forty nights;"

In the days of Joseph there were seven years of plenty which were followed by seven years of famine. (Genesis 41:10 & 30)

Seven things are connected with the complete destruction of Jericho, "And they utterly destroyed all that was in the city, (1) both man and (2) woman, (3) young and (4) old, and (5) ox, and (6) sheep, and (7) ass, with the edge of the sword." (Joshua 6:21) Before the walls of the city fell down, the children of Israel marched around the city seven days and seven times of the seventh day. (Joshua 6:3-5)

Jesus spoke seven times from the cross. The seventh statement was, "It is finished:" "When Jesus therefore had received the vinegar, he said, It is finished: and he bowed his head, and gave up the ghost." (John 19:30)

New Birth
"EIGHT"

Eight is the number of the new birth. It is twice four, the number for the first creation. In the new birth one becomes a new creature.

In our Lord's conversation with Nicodemus on the subject of the new birth the word "born" occurs eight times. (John 3:3-8) In the statement, "So is every one that is born of the

Spirit." the word "born" occurs the eighth and last time. The original Greek uses eight words. There are eight Greek words in the statement, "and that which is born of the Spirit is spirit." (John 3:6) Paul used eight Greek words when he said, "And last of all he was seen of me also, as of one born out of due time." (I Corinthians 15:8) There are also eight Greek words in the statement, "and every one that loveth is born of God," (I John 4:7)

Colossians 3:9 shows eight things are connected with the new man, "Lie not one to another, seeing that ye have put off the old man with his deeds; And have put on the new man, which is renewed in knowledge after the image of him that created him: Where there is neither *Greek*, nor *Jew*, *circumcision* nor *uncircumcision*, *Barbarian*, *Scythian*, *bond* nor *free*: but Christ is all, and in all."

A believer receives new birth through the divine nature of God. "Whereby are given unto us exceeding great and precious promises: that by these ye might be partakers of the divine nature, having escaped the corruption that is in the world through lust. And beside this, giving all diligence, add to your *faith virtue*; and to virtue *knowledge*; and to knowledge *temperance*; and to temperance *patience*; and to patience *godliness*; and to godliness *brotherly kindness*; and to brotherly kindness *charity*." (II Peter 1:4-7)

There were eight people in the ark for the purpose of replenishing the earth after the flood. (I Peter 3:20)

David, the second king of Israel, was the eighth son of Jesse. (I Samuel 17:12-14)

Isaac, Abraham's second-born son, was a child of promise. The children of God are children of promise. "Now we, brethren, as Isaac was, are the children of promise." Isaac, the second-born, was typical of those who possess the New Birth. He was circumcised when he was eight days old, "And Abraham circumcised his son Isaac being eight days old, as God had commanded him." (Genesis 21:4) There are exactly eight Greek words in this statement, "Now we brethren, as Isaac was, are the children of promise." To be a child of promise you must have the new birth. (Galatians 4:28)

In Exodus 25:8, God said to Moses, "And let them make me a sanctuary; that I may dwell among them." The tabernacle represented a dwelling place for God among His people. God dwells in one who is born again. "Hereby know we that we dwell in him, and he in us, because he hath given us of his Spirit." (I John 4:13) There were eight groups encamped around the tabernacle: four in the outward and four in the inward. In Numbers 1:52 and 53, God said, "And the children of Israel shall pitch their tents, every man by his own camp, and every man by his own standard, throughout their hosts. But the Levites shall pitch round about the tabernacle of testimony, that there be no wrath upon the congregation of the children of Israel: and the Levites shall keep the charge of the tabernacle of Testimony." Ephesians 2:3 declares that we "were by nature the children of wrath," With the statement, "that there be no wrath upon the congregation of the children of Israel:" follow the meaning of Ephesians 2:3, and you'll see what God meant in Numbers 1:52 and 53. The four groups on the outward arrangement represent the unsaved man who is by nature a child of wrath. When four more groups are added to the camp and are placed next to the tabernacle, this is the new birth which saved man from the wrath of God. The second chapter of Numbers tells us about the four outward groups which had to pitch outside the tabernacle. In Numbers 2:1 and 2:3-7, we find the camp of Judah with three tribes on the East. In Numbers 2:10-16, we find the camp of Rueben with three tribes on the South. In Numbers 2:18-24 it is stated that the camp of Ephraim with three tribes was on the West, and in verses 25-31 it is stated that Dan with three tribes was on the North. This makes four camps which were pitched afar off. This outward arrangement was given first. With this outward arrangement of four camps, there were four more groups. These were the tribes of the Levites. This arrangement is given in the third chapter of Numbers. The family of the Gershonites was on the West. (Numbers 3:23-26) The families of the Kohathites was on the

South. (Numbers 3:29-32) The families of the Merarites were in the North. (Numbers 3:33-35) In the East was Aaron, Moses and the sons of Aaron which made eight groups in all: four in the outward arrangement and four in the inward. In the center of the whole camp was the Tabernacle, God's dwelling place, among the people, picturing Jesus in the heart of the born-again person, "the hope of glory" as in Colossians 1:27.

In Ezekiel 36:26, God said to Israel, "A new heart also will I give you, and a new spirit will I put within you:" When three, the resurrection, is added to five, grace, they total eight, which is the number for the new birth. This shows how perfect the Bible system of numbers fit together to form a God-perfect numeral pattern.

Fruit of the Spirit
"NINE"

The fruit of the Spirit follows the new birth just as logically as number eight precedes nine. Jesus said, "make the tree good, and his fruit good;" The tree, man, is made good by the new birth and the good fruit which is the fruit of the Spirit. As a result of the new birth, "A good man out of the good treasure of the heart bringeth forth good things:" (Matthew 12:33-35) The fruit does not produce the tree; the tree is the result of a good seed. Man is not made good by doing good, he must have a good heart. He must be born again and then good works will follow, "by grace are ye saved through faith; and that not of yourselves: it is the gift of God: Not of works, lest any man should boast. For we are his workmanship, created in Christ Jesus unto good works," (Ephesians 2:8-10) Creation unto good works takes place in someone who is born again, which is represented by the number eight. Number nine, the fruit of the Spirit, follows after

51

the new birth. "the fruit of the Spirit is *love, joy, peace, longsuffering, gentleness, goodness, faith, meekness, temperance*: against such there is no law." (Galatians 5:22 & 23) The nine gifts of the Spirit are: "For to one is given by the Spirit the *word of wisdom*; to another the *word of knowledge* by the same Spirit; To another *faith* by the same Spirit; to another the gifts of *healing* by the same Spirit; To another the *working of miracles*; to another *prophecy*; to another *discerning of Spirits*; to another *divers kinds of tongues*; to another *interpretation of tongues*: But all these worketh that one and the selfsame Spirit, dividing to every man severally as he will." (I Corinthians 12:8-11)

"Now concerning spiritual gifts, brethren, I would not have you ignorant." (I Corinthians 12:1) Up until Paul says that these worketh the selfsame Spirit, there are nine references to the Spiritual gifts of God. Jesus spoke nine beatitudes in His sermon on the Mount. (Matthew 5:4-11) A comparison of those nine beatitudes with the nine fruits of the Spirit in Galatians 5:22 and 23 will show a striking similarity. In the west end of the Court of the Tabernacle, there were nine spaces between the pillars, "And for the breadth of the court on the west side shall be hangings of fifty cubits: their pillars ten, and their sockets ten." (Exodus 27:12) If the reader would make ten straight lines on a piece of paper, he would find there are nine spaces between the lines. The hanging cross at the west end was 50 cubits in length and five cubits in height. (Exodus 27:18) Number 50 is associated with the Holy Ghost, Who descended on Pentecost 50 days after the resurrection of Jesus Christ. So the number of spaces, which is nine, is connected with the hanging, which was 50 cubits long, and represents the work of the Holy Ghost, and the nine is the fruit of the Spirit. Now let us study how these numbers in the hanging of the west end of the court work together. "The length of the court shall be an hundred cubits, and the breadth fifty every where, and the height five cubits of fine twined linen, and their sockets of brass." (Exodus 27:18) Here is shown that there are nine spaces in the hanging of 50 cubits on ten pillars. When all the numbers from one to nine are added the sum is 45. The height of the hanging was five cubits. When this five is added to the 45, the sum is 50, which was the number of cubits in the hanging cross at the west end of the tabernacle. This is the conclusion that nine is the number for the fruit of the Spirit.

Law
"TEN"

The number ten represents the Law. There are ten commandments in the law. (Exodus 20:3-17) The tenth reference to Israel's Egyptian bondage came just before the first commandment. "I am the Lord thy God, which have brought thee out of the land of Egypt, out of the house of bondage." (Exodus 20:2) This is the tenth reference to Israel's Egyptian bondage. The next word after bondage in this place is the first word of the ten commandments. Those ten references to Israel's bondage are found in Genesis 15:13 and 14; Exodus 1:14; twice in 2:23; 6:5; 6:6; 6:9; 13:2; 13:14; and the tenth in 20:2.

Abraham took the bondwoman for his wife after being ten years in Canaan. Paul explains that Hagar represented the law, "And Sarai Abram's wife took Hagar her maid the Egyptian, after Abram had dwelt ten years in the land of Canaan, and gave her to her husband Abram to be his wife." (Genesis 16:3) "Tell me, ye that desire to be under the law, do ye not hear the law? For it is written, that Abraham had two sons, the one by a bondmaid, the other by a freewoman. But he who was of the bondwoman was born after the flesh; but he of the freewoman was by promise. Which things are an allegory: for these are the two covenants; the one from the mount Sinai, which gendereth to bondage which is Agar."

(Galatians 4:21-25)

The tenth time the word "sin" is found in I John is where it is said, "Whosoever committeth sin transgresseth also the law:" (NOTE: The word "sin" occurs in I John 2:2 and it's italicized, added by the translators.)

Exodus 26:1-3 shows there were ten linen curtains in the Tabernacle, "Moreover thou shalt make the tabernacle with ten curtains of fine twined linen, and blue, and purple, and scarlet: with cherubims of cunning work shall thou make them. The length of one curtain shall be eight and twenty cubits, and the breadth of one curtain four cubits: and every one of the curtains shall have one measure." The ten curtains represent the law which Jesus Christ took out of the way and nailed to His cross, thus bringing grace to both Jew and Gentile. Number five is grace. "For he is our peace, who hath made both one, and hath broken down the middle wall of partition between us; Having abolished in his flesh the enmity, even the law of commandments contained in ordinances; for to make in himself of twain one new man, so making peace; And that he might reconcile both unto God in one body by the cross, having slain the enmity thereby:" (Ephesians 2:14-16)

The ten curtains were grouped together, five and five, and the five narrow curtains were perhaps sewed together to make a broad curtain and vice versa. Then there were 50 taches of gold, "And thou shalt make fifty taches of gold, and couple the curtains together with the taches: and it shall be one tabernacle." (Exodus 26:6) "And thou shalt hang up the vail under the taches," (Exodus 26:33) In the ten curtains coming over the tabernacle and the two broad curtains, making five each meeting at the veil, there is a picture of the ten commandments being taken out of the way and nailed to the cross. As a result, grace was brought to both the Jews and Gentiles. This is seen in the two fives and the two broad curtains, each made of five narrow ones hanging together with 50 taches. The overall picture shows the Jews and the Gentiles meeting at the cross of Jesus, joined together by the

Holy Ghost, Who is number 50, and made one people.

In Romans 4:15 it is said, "the law worketh wrath:" In the works of the flesh, as listed in Galatians 5:19-21, the tenth one is wrath.

Christ was conceived during the law, "But when the fulness of the time was come, God sent forth his Son, made of a woman, made under the law, To redeem them that were under the Law, that we might receive the adoption of sons." (Galatians 4:4 & 5) The Passover Lamb, which was a type of Christ (I Corinthians 5:7), was taken upon the tenth day of the month. (Exodus 12:3)

The law provided for a kinsman to redeem the property of one who had to sell his property because of poverty. And when Boaz redeemed the property of Elimelech, and his two sons he took ten men of the elders of the city to be witnesses for him. (Ruth 4:1-11) Here we see the righteousness of God being witnessed by the law and the prophets. (For further references read Romans 3:21.)

The following scriptures pertaining to the law have exactly ten Greek words in them. "Think not that I am come to destroy the law, or the prophets:" (Matthew 5:17) "For all the prophets and the law prophesied until John." (Matthew 11:13) "The scribes and the Pharisees sit in Moses' seat:" (Matthew 23:2) "Take ye him, and judge him according to your law." (John 18:31) "Except ye be circumcised after the manner of Moses, ye cannot be saved." (Acts 15:1)

"That it was needful to circumcise them, and to command them to keep the law of Moses." (Acts 15:5) "Therefore by the deeds of the law there shall no flesh justified in his sight:" (Romans 3:20) "Where is boasting then? It is excluded. By what law?" This statement of ten Greek words is followed by five Greek words. "Nay: but by the law of faith." (Romans 3:27) "But Israel, which followed after the law of righteousness, hath not attained to the law of righteousness." (Romans 9:31) "Wherefore? Because they sought it not by faith, but as it were by the works of the law." (Romans 9:32) "For it is written in the law of Moses, Thou shalt not muzzle the mouth of the ox that treadeth out the corn." (I Corinthians 9:9)

"Is the law then against the promises of God? God forbid:" (Galatians 3:21) "For all the law is fulfilled in one word," (Galatians 5:14) And when the words "Thou shalt love thy neighbor as thyself." were added there are 16 words: 16 is the number for love. It often takes two or more English words to translate a Greek verb. There are always more words than Greek in many of the Bible verses. Since most of the learned Bible readers understand Greek structure, there is no reason to go into further explanation.

Judgment
"ELEVEN"

Eleven is the number for judgment. Judgment follows after a broken law and ten signifies the law.

There were eleven judgments on Egypt in the days of Moses and Aaron. The Lord said to Moses, "Wherefore say unto the children of Israel, I am the Lord, and I will bring you out from under the burdens of the Egyptians, and I will rid you out of their bondage, and I will redeem you with a stretched out arm, and with great judgments:" (Exodus 6:6) The judgments and their locations are the plague of blood, Exodus 7:19-21; the plague of frogs, Exodus 8:1-7; the plague of lice, Exodus 8:16-17; the plague of boils, and blain, Exodus 9:8-11; the plague of hail, Exodus 9:22-25; the plague of locusts, Exodus 10:12-25; the plague of darkness, Exodus 10:21-23; the death of the firstborn, Exodus 12:29-30; the overthrow at the Red Sea, Exodus 14:24-28. The judgment of the flood came upon the world in the 11th generation. The generations are Adam, Seth, Enos, Cainan, Mahalaleel, Jared, Enoch, Methuselah, Lamech, Noah and his sons, Shem, Ham and Japheth. (Genesis 5:1-31) Noah's sons were born before the flood making them the last generation on the earth. Noah pronounced judgment upon Canaan, Ham's son, because of Ham's disrespect for his father when he looked upon Noah's nakedness which was his wife. (Leviticus 18:8 & 20:11) Noah said, "Cursed be Canaan; a servant of servants shall he be unto his brethren." (Genesis 9:20-25) Canaan, upon whom this judgment was pronounced, has 11 sons. "And Canaan begat (1) Sidon his firstborn, and (2) Heth, And the (3) Jebusite, and the (4) Amorite, and the (5) Girgasite, And the (6) Hivite, and the (7) Arkite, and the (8) Sinite, And the (9) Arvadite, and the (10) Zemarite, and the (11) Hamathite: and afterward were the families of the Canaanites spread abroad." (Genesis 10:15-18) Was it a mere coincidence that Canaan, upon whom Judgment was passed, had 11 sons, no more and no less? Here you'll notice that the 11th in the list was the Hamathite. No doubt this son of Canaan was named for Ham, the father of Canaan, and whose disrespect for his father brought on the judgment. Was it accidental that the 11th one was named after Ham, or did a Divine mind so arrange it?

God pronounced judgment and complete destruction on the house of Esau because of the unkind treatment of that people toward the Children of Israel. (Obadiah 1:8-18) In Genesis 36:40-43, there is found the names of the 11 dukes in the family of Esau, "And these are the names of the dukes that came of Esau, according to their families, after their places, by their names; duke *Timnah*, duke *Alvah*, duke *Jetheth*, Duke *aholibamah*, duke *Elah*, duke *Pinon*, Duke *Kenaz*, duke *Teman*, duke *Mibzar*, Duke *Magdiel*, duke *Iram*: these be the dukes of Edom, according to their habitations in the land of their possession: he is Esau the father of the Edomites." These genealogies are a part of the scripture which is given by inspiration of God, and they are profitable for doctrine. When studied in the light of the Bible numbers, they glow with meaning.

In Numbers 15:32-35, there is a record of a man who brought judgment upon himself by breaking the law of the

Sabbath. "And while the children of Israel were in the wilderness, they found a man that gathered sticks upon the sabbath day. And they that found him gathering sticks brought him unto Moses and Aaron, and unto all the congregation. And they put him in ward, because it was not declared what should be done to him. And the Lord said unto Moses, The man shall be surely put to death:"

The Sabbath day was the seventh day of the week. The commandment concerning the Sabbath was the fourth commandment. When the numbers seven and four are added together they total 11, for the judgment that man brought upon himself by breaking the law of the Sabbath. This passage shall be studied again with the number 23, which is death.

At Kadesh, sometimes called Kadesh-Barnea, the Israelites brought judgment upon themselves by refusing to go up and possess the promised land. (Numbers 13:25, 14:1-34) They were turned back to wander 40 years in the wilderness. Deuteronomy 1:2 states, "There are eleven days' journey from Horeb by the way of Mount Seir unto Kadesh-barnea." These 11 days of journey brought Israel to the place of judgment.

Isaiah foretold the judgment that would come unto Judah by naming 11 different kinds of men, "For, behold, the Lord, the Lord of hosts, doth take away from Jerusalem and from Judah the stay and the staff, the whole stay of bread, and the whole stay of water, (1) The mighty man, and (2) the man of war, (3) the judge, and (4) the prophet, and (5) the prudent, and (6) the ancient, (7) The captain of fifty, and (8) the honorable man, and (9) the counsellor, and (10) the cunning artificer, and (11) the eloquent orator." (Isaiah 3:1-3)

This judgment which Isaiah foretold came in the 11th year of the reign of Zedekiah, the last king of Judah. "Zedekiah was one and twenty years old when he began to reign, and he reigned eleven years in Jerusalem. And his mother's name was Hamutal the daughter of Jeremiah of Libnah. And he did that which was evil in the eyes of the Lord, according to all that Jehoiakim had done. For through the anger of the Lord it came to pass in Jerusalem and Judah, till he had cast them out from his presence, that Zedekiah, rebelled against the king of Babylon. And it came to pass in the ninth year of his reign, in the tenth month, in the tenth day of the month, that Nebuchadnezzar king of Babylon came, he and all his army, against Jerusalem, and pitched against it, and built forts against it round about. So the city was besieged unto the eleventh year of king Zedekiah. And in the fourth month, in the ninth day of the month, the famine was sore in the city, so that there was no bread for the people of the land." (Here Isaiah's prophecy was fulfilled.) (Jeremiah 52:1-6) "Then the city was broken up, and all the men of war fled, and went forth out of the city by night by the way of the gate between the two walls, which was by the king's garden; (now the Chaldeans were by the city round about:) and they went by the way of the plain. But the army of the Chaldeans pursued after the king, and overtook Zedekiah in the plains of Jericho; and all his army was scattered from him. Then they took the king, and carried him up into the king of Babylon to Riblah in the land of Hamath; where he gave judgment upon him." (Jeremiah 52:7-9)

Dinah was the 11th child born unto Jacob, and her name means judgment. (Genesis 20:32, 30:21)

In Ezekiel 26:1-14 the prophet Ezekiel, in the 11th year of his prophecy, foretold the judgment that would come on Tyrus, or Enoch's prophecy of judgment. In Jude, verses 14 and 15, judgment again is connected with 11. Remember here Enoch's prophecy of judgment and how it has to do with the number 11. "And Enoch also, the seventh from Adam, prophesied of these, saying, Behold, the Lord cometh with ten thousands of his saints, To execute judgment upon all, and to convince all that are *ungodly* among them of all their *ungodly* deeds which they have *ungodly* committed, and of all their hard speeches which *ungodly* sinners have spoken against him." The word "ungodly" is found four times. Enoch, who did the prophesying, was the seventh from Adam, and when four is added to seven the sum is 11, the number for the judgment which Enoch foretold.

Noah's judgment (Hebrews 11:7) tells that in preparing the ark Noah condemned the world. God gave to Noah the instruction as how to build the ark, "Thus did Noah; according to all that God commanded him, so did he." (Genesis 6:22) The name of Noah occurs the 11th time in this place and this again connects number 11 with judgment.

More than 50 passages can be found in the New Testament where just 11 Greek words or 11 Greek letters are connected with judgment. Following are three examples: John 3:18, "He that believeth on him is not condemned: but he that believeth not is condemned already, because he hath not believed in the name of the only begotten Son of God." The Greek translation of this scripture reads, "But he that believeth not already has been judged." In the words, "already hath been judged," remembering that this is in the original Greek, there are exactly 11 Greek letters. They are "ADA KEKRIT AI." The 11 Greek words are the reason why the unbeliever has already been judged. James 3:1, "My brethren, be not many masters, knowing that we shall receive the greater condemnation." This statement has 11 Greek words. The two Greek words for the greater judgment (here again the word "judgment" is used from the original Greek) have 11 Greek letters.

At the beginning of the discussion of number 11 there is shown 11 judgments on Egypt, and the 11th was the overthrow at the Red sea. In Hebrews 11:29 we read, "By faith they passed through the Red sea as by dry land: which the Egyptians assaying to do were drowned." In the words "were drowned" there are exactly 11 Greek letters. So the judgment, number 11, that came on Egypt is spelled with 11 Greek letters, and 11 is the number for judgment.

This concludes number 11. There are numerous other passages in both the Old and New Testaments proving num-

60

ber 11 as judgment, but this should suffice as the best general summarization.

Divine Power, Rule or Authority "TWELVE"

Twelve is Divine Power, Rule or Authority, making it the most important number in the system. It is the next number after 11, which is Judgment, and God has the power to pass judgment on all of His subjects. Twelve is three times four: three is for resurrection, and four is creation. Therefore, 12 would be an expression of the rule of the tribute "God over Creation." Without resurrection, we have no God over Creation. The divine order of things is always logical, simple and plain when seen clearly.

The first passage which I would like to call to your attention is in Daniel 4:29-32, "At the end of twelve months he walked in the palace of the kingdom of Babylon. The king spake, and said, Is not this great Babylon, that I have built for the house of the kingdom by the might of my power, and for the honour of my majesty? While the word was in the king's mouth, there fell a voice from heaven, saying, O king Nebuchadnezzar, to thee it is spoken; The kingdom is departed from thee. And they shall drive thee from men, and thy dwelling shall be with the beasts of the field: they shall make thee to eat grass as oxen, and seven times shall pass over thee, until thou know that the most High ruleth in the kingdom of men,. and giveth it to whomsoever he will." All that came upon king Nebuchadnezzar at the end of 12 months. Notice how long Nebuchadnezzar walked in the palace of Babylon. In Daniel 4:30-32, the number 12 is connected with the rule of the most High God.

Jesus connected His rule with the rule of the 12 Apostles, "when the Son of man shall sit in the throne of his glory, ye

61

also shall sit upon twelve thrones, judging the twelve tribes of Israel." (Matthew 19:28)

In I Kings 18:22-44, there is an account of Elijah's contest with the prophets of Baal. He had four barrels of water poured over his sacrifice three times. This makes 12 barrels of water poured over the altar. "And it came to pass at the time of the offering of the evening sacrifice, that Elijah the prophet came near, and said, Lord God of Abraham, Isaac, and of Israel, let it be known this day that *THOU ART GOD IN ISRAEL*, and that I am thy servant, and that I have done all these things *AT THY WORD*." (Verse 36) The number 12 in this connection represents the divine power or rule in Israel, and over the forces of nature.

After Jesus had fed the 5000 with the five barley loaves and two fishes, He gathered up 12 baskets of the fragments which remained. These 12 baskets signify the divine power by which the miracle was wrought. After Jesus had fed the 4000, they gathered up seven baskets. The words "seven baskets" are spelled with 12 Greek letters which represent divine power. (Matthew 15:35-38)

In Ephesians 1:19-20, Paul speaks of the mighty power of God that He wrought in Christ when He raised Him from the dead. In speaking of His death and resurrection, Jesus said, "But he answered and said unto them, An evil and adulterous generation seeketh after a *sign*; and there shall no *sign* be given to it, but the *sign* of the prophet Jonas: For as Jonas was *three* days and *three* nights in the whale's belly; so shall the Son of man be *three* days and *three* nights in the heart of the earth." (Matthew 12:39-40) Jesus used the number three four times while speaking of His death and resurrection as a sign to Israel. Three is the number for resurrection. He could have said, "as Jonas was three days and nights," that would have told us how long He would be dead. But He used 12, represented by three times four to set forth the divine power by which He was raised.

The 12th time Noah's Ark is mentioned is where it is said that they went in by commandment, "And they went in unto

Noah into the ark, two and two of all flesh, wherein is the breath of life. And they that went in, went in male and female of all flesh, as God had commanded him: and the Lord shut him in." (Genesis 7:15-16) The number 12 shows the divine authority that sent them into the ark.

The 12th time the name of Noah is mentioned is found where God called him to come into the ark, "And the Lord said unto Noah, Come thou and all thy house into the ark;" (Genesis 7:1) In this scripture Noah's name is mentioned the 12th time, and the ark is mentioned the eighth time, and there were eight persons in Noah's house.

God appointed 12 months to the year, 12 hours to the day, and 12 hours to the night: "Jesus answered, Are there not twelve hours in the day?" (John 11:9) In Genesis 1:16 we find that the sun is to rule the day and the moon to rule the night: "And God made two great lights; the greater light to rule the day, and the lesser light to rule the night:" God gave the sun rule for 12 hours and the moon rule for 12 hours.

God spoke to Job about the 12 signs of the Zodiac and their dominion rule over the earth, "Canst thou bind the sweet influence of Pleiades, or loose the bands of Orion? Canst thou bring forth Mazzaroth in his season? or canst thou guide Arcturus with his sons? Knowest thou the ordinances of heaven? canst thou set the dominion [rule] thereof in the earth?" (Job 38:31-33) The word "Mazzaroth" is rendered "The twelve signs" in the margin; Moffatt translates this word as "The signs of the Zodiac." The Bible dictionary renders in the same way. The 12 signs of the Zodiac did not have their origin with man, but with God. There are many, including myself, who state that the Astrologers do not know the origin of the 12 constellations, nor why they are called signs of Zodiac. In their song of victory, Deborah said, "They fought from heaven; the stars in their courses fought against Sisera. The river Kishon swept them away," (Judges 5:20-21) Evidently the influence of the stars brought down rain at the right time to cause the flood in the small river Kishon which caused Sisera's army to be swept away. God had said, "I will draw unto thee to the river Kishon Sisera, the captain of Jabin's army, with his chariots and his multitude; and I will deliver him into thine hand." (Judges 4:7) Our God controls the stars and fixes their dominion over the earth. He knew just when to draw the army of Sisera to the river of Kishon at the time of the 12 signs of the Zodiac to bring the flood, though Deborah could say that the stars in their courses fought against Sisera.

The number 12 is mentioned many times concerning the New Jerusalem descending out of the heavens. If you've studied Revelation, this will certainly be brought to your mind. There are 12 gates and the gates are 12 pearls, and there are 12 kinds of precious stones representing the 12 apostles. The city measures 12,000 furlongs in every direction. The wall is 144 cubits high, which is 12 times 12. The tree of life had 12 manner of fruits and bore its fruit every month of all 12 months. If this hasn't convinced you of the Divine Authority of God and His Power, nothing will.

The 12th time the name of Abraham occurs is where it says, "And the Lord appeared unto Abram, and said, Unto thy seed will I give this land:" (Genesis 12:7) The seed of Abraham possessed the land by divine authority and will again possess it with divine rule.

The tabernacle, which was built for a dwelling place for God among His people (Exodus 25:8), was 12 cubits wide. Many have said the width was only ten cubits, but with close examination you'll notice the Bible is correct. In Ezekiel 41:1 we read, "Afterwards he brought me to the temple, and measured the posts, six cubits broad on the one side, and six cubits broad on the other side, which was the breadth of the tabernacle." (Two times six equals 12.) The boards stood up, and they were a cubit and a half wide. (Exodus 26:14-16) There were eight boards in the back of the Tabernacle, "And they shall be eight boards, and their sockets of silver, sixteen sockets; two sockets under one board," (Exodus 26:25) Eight times one and a half are 12 cubits. It would be impossible to make a structure ten cubits wide out of boards a cubit and a half wide. One and a half does not divide evenly into ten, but it does into 12. Thus the tabernacle was 12 cubits wide, representing divine power and authority.

Twelve Greek letters are connected with divine authority many times. Many of us are aware of the fact that the average reader is not learned in the Greek language. There are many truths hidden in the language as was written from the beginning. The Bible number system can prove the virgin birth of Jesus Christ was brought about by divine power. We shall see that the writing of the scripture and the divine power is proven in Bible numbers. Today so much effort is being expended to discredit the virgin birth of Jesus. We need to know the truth, and the Bible numbers represent a line of argument which no one can wave aside by saying, "That was just an opinion of those who wrote the Bible."

Please mark this in your Bible, "For he taught them as one having authority, and not as the scribes." (Matthew 7:29) This passage in Matthew has exactly 12 Greek words; the two words "having authority" have exactly 12 Greek letters.

"Thou couldest have no power at all against me, except it were given thee from above:" (John 19:11) There are 12 Greek words in this scripture. Authority given from above comes from God.

In John 3:35 we read, "The Father loveth the Son, and hath given all things into his hand." God had given all authority to His Son, Jesus Christ. Again, there are 12 Greek words. "Hath given all things", shows 12 Greek letters.

"All things were made by him; and without him was not any thing made" (John 1:3) Here again there are 12 Greek words. This shows that the divine power resided in Jesus Christ.

"In him was life; and the life was the light of men." (John 1:4) Again we find 12 Greek words which show the power that can give life.

"Then he arose, and rebuked the winds and the sea; and there was a great calm." (Matthew 8:26) This shows the power that Jesus has over the forces of nature. There are 12 Greek words in this passage.

The stilling of the winds and the waves produced wonder among the disciples, and they asked, "What manner of man is this, that even the winds and sea obey him!" (Matthew 8:27) Here are 12 Greek words that show our Lord's power and authority over the many forces of nature as used in verse 26, "Tote egertheis epetimnsen tois enemois kai ta thalassa kai egeneto galana megala." (Greek)

In Matthew 19:28 we read, "ye also shall sit upon twelve thrones, judging the twelve tribes of Israel." (Again there are 12 Greek words.)

"And they prayed, and said, Thou, Lord, which knowest the hearts of all men, shew whether of these two thou hast chosen," (Acts 1:24) Again 12 Greek words. They are connected with God's divine choice. God has the authority to choose whom He will.

"And he laid his hands on her: and immediately she was made straight, and glorified God." (Luke 13:13) This shows the power Jesus had over disease, and He used 12 Greek words to describe it.

"So then it is not of him that willeth, nor of him that runneth, but of God that sheweth mercy." (Romans 9:16) This also shows God's authority in blessing.

"Even so then at this present time also there is a remnant according to the election of grace." God only has the power to elect or choose and He used 12 Greek words to prove it. (Romans 11:5)

In Revelation 11:15, it says, "The kingdoms of the world are become the kingdoms of our Lord, and of his Christ;" We find another passage that has to do with the authority of God and of Christ and it also has 12 Greek words.

We have reviewed many scriptures that prove 12 to be the number connected with His divine power and authority. The words in the original Greek language were arranged by God to count as 12.

Now we shall proceed to examine the scriptures which

have to do with the birth of Jesus. This is probably the most important association with the number 12.

The Virgin Birth

"And, behold, thou shalt conceive in thy womb, and bring forth a son, and shalt call his name JESUS." (Luke 1:31) There are exactly 12 Greek words in this statement. This is of such vast importance that I've listed the 12 words for you: (1) sullapsa (2) en (3) gastri (4) kai (5) texa (6) huion (7) kai (8) kaleseis (9) to (10) onoma (11) autou (12) jasoun. When Mary wanted to know how this thing should be, the angel said that the power of the Highest should overshadow her. Number 12 has been seen to be connected with the power of God again and again, and the 12 words spoken to Mary about conceiving and bringing forth a son show the divine power connected with the virgin birth of Jesus.

"For unto you is born this day in the city of David a Saviour, which is Christ the Lord." (Luke 2:11) This, too, has just 12 Greek words.

Galatians 4:4 states, "God sent forth his Son, made of a woman, made under the law." Here are 12 Greek words again.

Matthew 1:23 reads, "they shall call his name Emmanual, which being interpreted is, God with us." This statement also has 12 Greek words, and the words "God with us" have 12 Greek letters.

"And with out controversy great is the mystery of godliness: God was manifest in the flesh," (I Timothy 3:16) Again here are 12 Greek words. The virgin birth and incarnation of Jesus Christ has been proven through the divine system of numbers. Being connected with the number 12 shows that the birth of Jesus was brought about by the divine power, and not by natural process. Do you doubt this? Nineteen passages have been pointed out that had 12 Greek words connected with divine power of God. In two of these verses, 12 Greek letters were found representing the same, and five of these passages were connected with the birth of Jesus Christ.

As we go farther into the numbers you'll see how 12, representing divine power and authority, fits together in numbers. It will be seen that 23 is the number connected with death. In Acts 27:14-44, Luke gives the account of the shipwreck of Paul and his companions, and how, out of the 276 on the ship, all were saved from death. When they despaired for their lives, God sent His angel to tell Paul that they should all be saved from death. Based upon the authority of God's Word, Paul told his companions they would all be saved from death. When 12, the number for divine power or authority, is divided into 276, the number of companions on the ship, the total is 23, the number for death. When all the numbers from one to 23 are added together, they total 276, the number of companions on the ship. These numbers could not work like this if they weren't correct. Anyone who has had an account knows that the numbers have to balance or else there will be a discrepancy. There are no discrepancies in God's numbering system. They balance at every point.

This is the conclusion of 12, the Divine Power, Rule or Authority of God.

Sin, Rebellion or Depravity "THIRTEEN"

Sin, Rebellion, or Depravity is the number 13. The number 12 stood for divine authority, and to go against divine authority would be to sin or rebel.

There are 13 evil things in Mark 7:21-23, "For from within, out of the heart of man, proceed *evil thoughts, adulteries, fornications, murders, Thefts, coveteousness, wickedness, deceit, lasciviousness, an evil eye, blasphemy, pride, foolishness*: All these evil things come from within, and defile the man."

Jesus has listed 13 evil things which can come out of the heart of man which defiles them. He says the heart is the source of these evil things and man is corrupt at his very foundation from which all of his deeds, words, and thoughts are derived.

Please notice that the word "deceit," which is the eighth word in the list, is connected with our New Birth. Consider this in the light of what Paul says in Colossians 3:9-10, "Lie [Deceit] not one to another, seeing that ye have put off the old man with his deeds; And have put on the new man, which is renewed in knowledge after the image of him that created him:" Deceit is to be expected from the man without new birth. It's in his heart, but deceit shouldn't be in the born again.

Blasphemy is the 11th word mentioned in the list; 11 is connected with judgment, and blasphemy brings God's judgment.

The 13th word in the list is foolishness. Solomon said, "Foolishness is bound in the heart of a child;" (Proverbs 22:15) Since 13 is the number for sin and depravity, this shows that the heart of a child is depraved and sinful.

In this list of evil things spoken of by Paul in Romans 1:29-31, the 13th one is "Haters of God": "the carnal mind is enmity against God: for it is not subject to the law of God, neither indeed can be." (Romans 8:7) Thirteen implies rebellion: "Twelve years they served Chedorlaomer, and in the thirteenth year they rebelled." (Genesis 14:4) Notice that rebellion is connected with the number 13.

Nimrod was the 13th generation from Adam through Ham; Ham was of the 11th generation. Cush, the son of Adam, from the 12th generation, became the father of Nimrod, making him the 13th generation. Then it is stated, "And the beginning of his kingdom was Babel," (Genesis 10:10) which led to the rebellion at the building of the tower of Babel. (Genesis 10:6-10) Nimrod is the 13th name given in the Lineage of Ham: (1) Ham, (2) Cush, (3) Mizraim, (4) Phut, (5) Canaan, (6) Seba, (7) Havilah, (8) Sebtah, (9) Raamah,

(10) Sebtechah, (11) Sheba, (12) Dedan, and (13) Nimrod. Then it is stated, "And the beginning of his kingdom was Babel,"

Haman, the enemy of the Jews, had a decree signed on the 13th day of the first month which was to have all the Jews put to death on the 13th day at the end of the year. "Then were the king's scribes called on the thirteenth day of the first month, and there was written according to all that Haman had commanded unto the king's lieutenants, and to the governors that were over every province, and to the rulers of every people of every province according to the writing thereof, and to every people after their language; in the name of King Ahasuerus was it written, and sealed with the king's ring. And the letters were sent by posts into all the king's province, to destroy, to kill, and to cause to perish, all Jews, both young and old, little children and women, in one day, even upon the thirteenth day of the twelfth month, which is the month of Adar, and to take the spoil of them for a prey." (Esther 3:12-13)

In the book of Revelation, the devil is symbolized as a dragon. (Revelation 12:9) While six is the number associated with the devil, we find the word "dragon" occurs 13 times in the book of Revelation. He is the author of sin and rebellion, and his name is found in the following places in Revelation: (1) 12:3, (2) 12:4, (3) and, (4) 12:7, (5) 12:9, (6) 12:13, (7) 12:16, (8) 12:17, (9) 13:2, (10) 13:4, (11) 13:11, (12) 16:13 and the 13th time in 20:2. The numbers one through 13 total 91, which we'll explore later.

The 13th time the name of Mordecai is found is where the king's servants said unto him, "Why transgressest thou the king's commandment?" (Esther 3:3) Jeremiah was called in the 13th year of Josiah's reign by prophecy, "a revolting and a rebellious heart; they are revolted and gone." (Jeremiah 5:23) "To whom the words of the Lord came in the days of Josiah the son of Amon king of Judah, in the thirteenth year of his reign." (Jeremiah 1:2) Moses called Israel a rebellious people. A few days before his death, he said unto them, "from the day that thou didst depart out of the land of Egypt, until ye came unto this place, ye have been rebellious against the Lord." (Deuteronomy 9:7) The words "rebel," "rebels" and "rebelled" are nouns, verbs and adjectives which are used 13 times concerning Israel's wilderness conduct. They are found in Numbers 14:9, 17:10, 20:10, 20:24, 24:14; Deuteronomy 1:26, 1:43, 9:7, 9:23, 9:24, two times in 31:27 and the 13th time in Psalm 78:8.

There were 21 sins recorded against Israel from Egypt to Jordan. Since this number will be needed to understand the numbers found in Numbers 3:39-48, I'm going to give you the location of each of them: Exodus 14:10, 15:23-24, 16:19-23, 16:1-3, 16:27-28, 17:1-4, 32:1-9; Leviticus 10:1-2, 24:10-14; Numbers 11:1-3, 11:10-35, 12:1-15, 14:1-11, 14:40-45, 15:32-36, 16:41-50, 20:1-6, 20:8-12, 21:4-9 and the 21st time is in Numbers 25:1-9. In Numbers 3:39-48 we find an account of the redemption of 273; it comes out exactly 21 times, which is the number of sins which have been listed above. The sins make redemption necessary. The five shekels which paid for the redemption represent the grace of God by which we have redemption from sin. In this case, 13 represents Israel's rebellious or sinful nature which led to 21 acts of disobedience. Man's depraved nature caused him to commit open acts of rebellion. Redemption, through the grace of God, is represented by the five shekels.

Let's examine the way these numbers fit together. When number 13 is subtracted from 21, which is the product of dividing 273 by 13, eight is the remainder which stands for new birth. Israel needed the new birth. Moses spoke of the new birth, "Circumcise therefore the foreskin of your heart, and be no more stiffnecked." (Deuteronomy 10:16)

In Ezekiel 36:26, God said to Israel, "A new heart also will I give you, and a new spirit will I put within you: and I will take away the stoney heart out of your flesh, and I will give you an heart of flesh."

Here is grace giving and taking away. When three, for the resurrection, is added to five, for grace, that makes eight for the new heart or new birth. This is one of the most beautiful pictures in the whole Bible. Let's take the prodigal son, another example of how the numbers work. We find in the case of the prodigal son that when he came to himself, he said, "I will arise and go to my father, and will say unto him, Father, I have sinned against heaven, and before thee," (Luke 15:18) Thirteen, representing the prodigal sin, subtract the five things which the father did and eight is left for the new birth. "And he arose, and came to his father. But when he was yet a great way off, his father (1) saw him, and (2) had compassion, (3) and ran, (4) and fell on his neck, and (5) kissed him." (Verse 22) Notice what follows: "But the father said to his servants, (1) Bring forth the best robe, and (2) put it on him; and (3) put a ring on his hand, and (4) shoes on his feet: And (5) bring hither the fatted calf, and (6) kill it; and (7) let us eat, and (8) be merry:"

NOW NOTICE THE REASON: "For this my son was dead, and is alive again; he was lost, and is found. And they began to be merry." (Luke 15:22-24) Number 13 represents the sin of the prodigal, and the five things the Father did represent grace; the eight things the Father commanded to be done represent the new birth by which men are made alive again.

Don't you love to study God's Word and know what it means? When five, eight and 13 are added they equal 26, which stands for the good news of the gospel. It was good news and an occasion of rejoicing when the prodigal returned and that gospel, when received in our lives, brings rejoicing.

The five things that were done are preceded by five Greek words which are translated "But when he was yet a great way off," These words are: (1) ETE (2) DE (3) AUTOU (4) MAKRAN (5) APECTONTOS. Who but the Lord could tell a story that would fit together like this? Instead of distracting from its beauty, the numbers make it glow with beauty and meaning.

Let's talk a moment about Ishmael and Isaac. In Galatians 4:21-23, Paul states that the son of the bondwoman, Ishmael, was born after the flesh, and the son of the freewoman, Isaac, was by promise. Then in Colossians 2:11, it states, "In whom ye are circumcised with the circumcision made without hands, in putting off the body of the sins of the flesh by the circumcision of Christ:" Ishmael, who was born after the flesh, was circumcised when he was 13 years of age. (Genesis 17:25) So the flesh is connected with Ishmael, and 13, the number for sin. His circumcision represents the putting off of the sins of the flesh. When one has put off the old man, he has put on the new man. Isaac, the second-born, was the new child. He was circumcised when eight days old. This number represents the new or second birth, and this is why the eight is connected with Isaac. The difference between the 13 connected with Ishmael and the eight connected with Isaac is five, which stands for grace. The grace of God makes the difference between one in the flesh and one born again.

In discussing the next number it will be seen that 14 is the number for salvation. Not only was there a difference connected with the number five in the circumcision of Ishmael and Isaac, but a difference of 14 years in their birth.

In Genesis 16:16 it is stated that Abram was 86 years old when Ishmael was born. In Genesis 21:5 it is stated that Abraham was 100 years old when Isaac was born. Now the difference between 86 and 100 is 14, which stands for salvation. Israel was saved out of Egypt on the 14th day of the month. (Exodus 12:18-27) This difference of 14 between the number salvation makes a difference in one after the flesh and the one who has the new birth.

The number connected with the two sons of Abraham will grow more marvelous as we go farther in the study of numbers.

Salvation or Deliverance
"FOURTEEN"

Fourteen is the number for salvation or deliverance. The one who is a sinner is in need of salvation. Thirteen represents sin, and the next number is 14, representing salvation or deliverance from sin. In Colossians 1:13, the Greek words which are translated "Who hath delivered us" (in the first part of Colossians 1:13), there are 14 Greek letters, the number for sin. Then the words, "from the power of darkness," have 23 letters, and 23 is the number for death, as shall be explained later. When God delivers, He delivers from sin and death. "For the law of the Spirit of life in Christ Jesus hath made me free from the law of sin and death." (Romans 8:2)

Israel was saved or delivered from Egyptian bondage on the 14th day of the month, "And it shall come to pass, when ye be come to the land which the Lord will give you, according as he hath promised, that ye shall keep this service. And it shall come to pass, when your children shall say unto you, What mean ye by this service? That ye shall say, It is the sacrifice of the Lord's passover, who passed over the houses of the children of Israel in Egypt, when he smote the Egyptians, and delivered our houses. And the people bowed the head and worshipped." (Exodus 12:25-27) "In the fourteenth day of the first month at even is the Lord's passover." (Leviticus 23:5) This shows that 14 is connected with deliverance, or the saving of the house of Israel.

In Jeremiah 33:1, the Lord came to the prophet Jeremiah the second time while he was shut up in prison. From the opening of this chapter to the 15th verse, the Lord uses "Praise God" and the personal pronoun "I" concerning Himself 14 times. Then said He, "In those days shall Judah be saved and Jerusalem shall dwell safely." Jeremiah 33:15-16 reads, "In those days, and at that time, will I cause the Branch of righteousness to grow up unto David; and he shall execute judgment and righteousness in the land. In those days shall Judah be saved, and Jerusalem shall dwell safely: and this is the name wherewith she shall be called, 'THE LORD OUR RIGHTEOUSNESS.' " The word "Saved" follows right after the Lord used the word "I" the 14th time. Please count for yourself and see if it is right! When God does a thing He does it right, and any mistake would be on my part; for without Spirit and Truth I would have gained nothing in the sight of man or God. By reading Acts 27:33-44, you will see that Paul and all on the ship with him were saved from the storm and the sea on the 14th day of the storm. This didn't just happen; God brought it to pass, because 14 stands for salvation. This revelation that Jesus showed me came easy for my understanding and proves the word in Spirit and Truth.

There was a difference of 14 years between Ishmael, who Paul said was born after the flesh, and Isaac, whom Paul said was a child of promise. (Galatians 4:23, 4:28; Genesis 16:16, 21:5) The number 14 stands for salvation, and salvation makes the difference between those in the flesh and the children of God who are the children of promise.

Romans 10:13 states, "For whosoever shall call upon the name of the Lord shall be saved." Take number 14, salvation, then add one through 14 and the total is 105. In Genesis 4:26, it is stated that when Enoch was born "then began men to call upon the name of the Lord." In Genesis 5:6 it is seen that number 105 is connected with the birth of Enoch. Anyone doubt this?

All of the numbers came through Jesus Christ. But you, my friend, can try to fabricate a system different from the one found in the Bible and you'll quickly despair. It would be impossible for any living creature to design a system like this and adjust it to the Bible from beginning to end. Jesus Christ Himself designed this system and put it in His book for us to use, and He pointed it out to me and I've got to bring it forth.

There is a passage of scripture that all children of God delight in quoting as evidence of their salvation. That passage is, "We know that we have passed from death unto life, because we love the brethren." (I John 3:14) This passage has 14 Greek words. The statement, "Who shall tell thee words whereby thou and all thy house shall be saved." (Acts 11:14) has 14 Greek words. These are not isolated passages, but many other examples could be shown.

In Galatians 1:13-14, Paul speaks of his former bondage to the law. In Galatians 1:15-16 he tells us about salvation. Following this is the opening of the next chapter and he speaks about going up to Jerusalem. Paul said, "Then fourteen years after I went up again to Jerusalem with Barnabas, and took Titus with me also. And I went up by revelation, and communication unto them that gospel which I preach among the Gentiles," You see 14 years (Acts 15:1-10) show that his trip was made to confer with the Apostles and Elders concerning the question of circumcision being essential to salvation, as some false brethren from Judea had been teaching. Paul had been saved for 14 years before he went with Barnabas and Titus to Jerusalem to confer with the Apostles about salvation.

The penitent thief was saved on the 14th day of the month. If you'll read Luke 22:4, Luke 23:46 and then read I Corinthians 11:23, you'll see that Christ observed the Passover in the evening of the morning of the same day as He was crucified and died. Let it be kept in mind that in the Bible a day was from the one evening to the next evening. "And the evening and the morning were the first day." The Passover was in the evening of the 14th day. Christ kept the Passover in the evening of the 14th day and was crucified the morning of the same day, and before the day ended He had died. The day Christ was crucified two thieves were also crucified. (Matthew 27:28 & Luke 23:32-43) That day the penitent thief called upon Jesus, and said, "Lord, remember me when thou comest into the kingdom." (Luke 23:42) Romans 10:13 states, "For whosoever shall call upon the name of the Lord shall be saved." Jesus replied to the thief's request, "verily I say unto thee, today shalt thou be with me in paradise." (Luke 23:42) So the thief was saved on the 14th day of the month, the day Jesus was crucified. Though the day of his salvation, the 14th, corresponds with the number for salvation, baptism had no part in this salvation because the death of Christ fell after the law of Moses. He did call upon the Lord that day, before the Lord's death, the fourteenth, and so he was saved that day by calling upon the name of the Lord. How marvelous that the Bible would connect his salvation with the number that stands for salvation before the death of Jesus on the 14th day of the month under the law of Moses.

Rest
"FIFTEEN"

Fifteen is the number for the rest of the believer. When we obtain salvation from sin we rest in Christ. It is seven, which was the day of rest connected with the old creation, and the number eight, which is the number for the new birth. The last Sabbath day before the abolishment of the law by the crucifixion of Jesus was the seventh day of the previous week. Eight days after that Sabbath, Jesus rose again. The Sabbath day Jesus was in the grave was not to be counted, because the Law had been abolished then.

Israel had three rest days in the 15th of the month. The first one was the 15th day of the first month, "In the fourteenth day of the first month at even is the Lord's passover. And on the fifteenth day of the same month is the feast of unleavened bread unto the Lord: seven days ye must eat unleavened bread. In the first day ye shall have an holy convocation: ye shall do no servile work therein." (Leviticus 23:5-7) The feast of the unleavened bread began on the 15th day and ran for seven days. On the first of these days, which was on the 15th day, they rested from work. Now the second rest day was the 15th day of the seventh month. "Speak unto the children of Israel, saying, The fifteenth day of this seventh month shall be the feast of tabernacles for seven days unto the Lord. On the first day shall be an holy convocation: ye shall do no servile work therein." (Leviticus 23:34-35)

Now the third rest day was on the 15th of the 12th month. "But the Jews that were at Shushan assembled together on the thirteenth day thereof, and on the fourteenth day thereof; and on the fifteenth day of the same they rested, and made it a day of feasting and gladness." (Esther 9:18) By reading Esther 9:20-21, we find that this was the month of Adar, which was the 12th month. The day of rest was on the 15th day of the month. By adding the numbers of months 1, 7, and 12, we get 20, which is the number for redemption. So the number 15 stands for the rest of the redeemed. If you'll add 15 and 20 the total is 35, which is the number for hope. It has been seen that three is the number for the resurrection, and there were three days of rest.

Galatians 1:13-14, Paul tells of his former bondage to the law, and in the next three verses he tells of his salvation and his trip to Arabia and back to Damascus. In the next verse, he said, "Then after three years I went up to Jerusalem to see Peter, and abode with him fifteen days." In Galatians 1:18 the number three is found, and the number 15 occurs three times. There are exactly 15 Greek words in this statement. There are 15 days, and in the words "fifteen days" there are exactly 15 Greek letters which are "AMERASDEKA-PENTE". First, there are 15 days; second, there are 15 words in the sentence; and, third, there are 15 letters in the words "fifteen days." This is exactly the number of rest days Israel had on the 15th day.

Grace brings the rest which is in Jesus. Five has been shown to be the number for grace. Add the numbers 1, 2, 3, 4, 5 and the sum is 15, the number for rest.

Our resurrection will usher the saints into our eternal rest. Multiply five, grace, by three, resurrection, and the product will be 15, representing rest.

Throughout the previous numbers we have mentioned that 23 stood for death. In Revelation 14:13, John said, "And I heard a voice from heaven saying unto me, Write, Blessed are the dead which die in the Lord from henceforth: Yea, saith the Spirit, that they may rest from their labours; and their works do follow them." In this expression, we have those in the Lord dying and resting, and when eight, for the new birth which those have who have died in the Lord, is subtracted from 23, the number for death, the remainder is 15, or rest. There are exactly eight Greek words in the statement, "Blessed are the dead who die in the Lord from henceforth:" This is the number for the new birth and shows that such have the new birth.

The name of Naomi is mentioned the 15th time in the book of Ruth. (Ruth 3:1) And the 15th time it is connected with rest. "Then Naomi her mother in law said unto her, My daughter, shall not I seek rest for thee, that it may be well with thee?" This rest came to Ruth through the kinsman, Boaz. The word "kinsman" is found 15 times in the book of Ruth. It is in 2:1, 2:20, 3:2, 3:9, twice in 3:12, four times in 3:13, 4:1, 4:3, 4:6, 4:8, and the last in 4:14. The book of Ruth is rich in Bible numbers as well as other things. There are many scriptures that could point to 15, but let's go on to 16.

Love
"SIXTEEN"

When the Lord saves a person, He gives him rest in his soul and furthers his love for God. Salvation, rest and love are all found in Psalm 116:1-8. The numbers for salvation, rest and love are 14, 15 and 16. "I LOVE the Lord, because he hath heard my voice and my supplications. Because he hath inclined his ear unto me, therefore will I call upon him as long as I live. The sorrows of death compassed me, and pains of hell gat hold upon me: I found trouble and sorrow. Then called I upon the name of the LORD; O LORD, I beseech thee, deliver my soul." (Psalm 116:1-4) "whosoever shall call upon the name of the Lord shall be saved." (Romans 10:13) "Then called I upon the name of the Lord; O Lord, I beseech thee, deliver my soul. Gracious is the Lord, and righteous; yea, our God is merciful. The Lord preserveth the simple: I was brought low, and he helped me. Return unto thy rest, O my soul; for the Lord hath dealt bountifully with thee. For thou hast delivered my soul from death, mine eyes from tears, and my feet from falling." (Psalm 116:4-8) I don't want to add to nor take away from any of the words of this book. I just wanted you to know that the words "delivered my soul;" I believe, mean "has saved my soul." In that passage, deliverance or salvation, rest and love are found. The reason the Psalmist gives for loving the Lord is that He has saved him and given him rest in his soul. The three grouped together are the same as 14, 15 and 16.

I discovered that 16 stood for love in I Corinthians 13:4-8, and I don't believe that you'll find it stronger anywhere else. When naming the church *God's Community Church of Charity*, certainly I had remembered I Corinthians 13. Let us look at the 13th chapter which pertains to love. It starts out in I Corinthians 13:4, "Charity, (1) suffereth long, and (2) is kind; (3) charity envieth not; (4) charity vaunteth not itself, (5) is not puffed up, (6) Doth not behave itself unseemingly, (7) seeketh not her own, (8) is not easily provoked, (9) thinketh no evil; (10) Rejoiceth not in iniquity, (11) but rejoiceth in the truth; (12) Beareth all things, (13) believeth all things, (14) hopeth all things, (15) endureth all things. (16) Charity never faileth:" Wouldn't you gather from this that 16 is love? Here are 16 adjectives describing charity or love. The seventh time the word charity is found in this chapter is where it says "Charity never faileth:" Seven stands for completeness or perfection. I John 4:12 says, "If we love one another, God dwelleth in us, and his love is perfected in us." The eighth time charity is mentioned is where it is said, "And now abideth faith, hope, charity, these three;" (I Corinthians 13:13) Eight is the number for the new birth which never fails and shall continually abide with God's children. John, writing to the elect Lady, said, "The elder unto the elect lady and her children, whom I love in the truth; and not I only, but also all they that have known the truth; For the truth's sake, which dwelleth in us, and shall be with us for ever." (II John 1:1) This is further proof that love never fails and that it shall remain with us. The ninth time charity is found is where it says, "but the greatest of these is charity." (Verse 13) Number nine is for the fruit of the Spirit as in Galatians 5:22-23. Love is the first of the nine fruits mentioned. The tenth time charity occurs is in I Corinthians 14:1 where Paul said, "Follow after charity." Number ten stands for the law; love is the fulfilling of the law. (Romans 13:10) The statement "follow after charity" has 16 Greek letters in it. In the west end of the tabernacle, it is said, "And they shall be eight boards, and their sockets of silver, sixteen sockets; two sockets under one board and two sockets under another board." (Exodus 26:25) John said, "every one that loveth is born of God," (I John 4:7) The eight boards represent the new birth. The 16 sockets in which they were set represent love in which the heart of the person with the new birth is grounded. In Ephesians 3:17 Paul speaks about the believer being rooted and grounded in love. Those eight boards in the west end of the tabernacle were fixed in 16 sockets by means of tenons (Exodus 26:17), and the sockets were set on or in the ground. How beautiful and harmonious is the Word of God. What could compare with the picture presented of the eight boards of the tabernacle set in or ground in 16 sockets showing the believer or born-again soul rooted and grounded in love (eight being the number for the new birth and 16 for love)? There is one peculiar passage which is a favorite with God's children and it has just 16 Greek words, "And we know that all things work together for good to them that love God, to them who are the called according to his purpose." (Romans 8:28) Another passage is Romans 5:5, which states, in part, "because the love of God is shed abroad in our hearts by the Holy Ghost which is given unto us." John 10:17, "Therefore doth my Father love me, because I lay down my life, that I might take it again." It was God's love for the world that caused Him to give His Son to die for the world, which leads us into number 17, the victory in Jesus.

Victory
"SEVENTEEN"

The next number, 17, is a marvelous number, and the way it works throughout the Bible is amazing.

Romans 8:35-39 lists 17 tests and trials we are faced with. God gives us the victory to conquer these, "Who shall separate us from the love of Christ? shall *tribulation*, or *distress*, or *persecution*, or *famine*, or *nakedness*, or *peril* or *sword*? As it is written, For thy sake we are killed all the day long; we are accounted as sheep for the slaughter. Nay, in all these things we are more than conquerors through him that loved us. For I am persuaded, that neither *death*, nor *life*, nor *angels*, nor *principalities*, nor *powers*, nor *things present*, nor *things to come*, Nor *height*, nor *depth*, nor *any other creature*, shall be able to separate us from the love of God, which is in Christ Jesus our Lord." Verse 35 mentions seven tests that cannot separate we who are saved from the love of Christ. We have complete security as a child of God. Verses 38 and 39 show ten instances in which we must be victorious through the love of God in Christ Jesus. The law cannot separate us from God's love. Why? Because God's children are dead to the law and are forever free from its demands. When the seven tests and trials in verse 35 are added to the ten in verses 38 and 39, they total 17. Paul states in verse 37, "in all these things we are more than conquerors through him that loved us." When we have dominion over these 17 trials and tests we have victory!

There are three titles in the Godhead, Father, Son and Holy Ghost, which is the Lord Jesus Christ, and these three are one. He is Lord of all, "above all, and through all, and in you all." (Ephesians 4:6) When the three titles are added to 14, salvation, the total is 17, for victory. The Father, Son and Holy Ghost are one: when you take the titles you'll find that resurrection is through God. To be resurrected, you must go down with Jesus and rise again with Him. When God's three titles are added to 14, salvation, the total is 17, for victory.

Jesus became victorious over death on the 17th day of the month. We have already discussed that Jesus died on the day of Passover, the 14th day of the month; three days later or on the 17th day He arose from the dead and became victorious over death, hell and the grave. "And having spoiled principalities and powers, he made a shew of them openly, triumphing over them in it." (Colossians 2:15)

When Jesus showed Himself to His disciples the third time after His resurrection there was a catch of 153 fish. (John 21:1-14) When 17, the number of the day of the month on which Jesus arose, is multiplied by three, for the resurrection, and by three again for the third time He showed Himself (17 x 3 x 3 = 153), the product is 153, the number of fish caught on this occasion. VICTORY!

I Samuel 17:40 states that David took five smooth stones when he went out to face Goliath. The stones represent grace, and we win our victory through grace. When David neared Goliath, he told him, "I come to thee in the name of the Lord of hosts, the God of the armies of Israel, whom thou hast defied." (I Samuel 17:45) David went out to meet his enemy in the name of authority and power. Twelve represents divine authority; add five stones which he took, and you'll have 17, for victory.

It works the same way in the case of Elijah — Elijah's contest with the prophets of Baal in I Kings 18:22-39. Elijah had four barrels of water poured on his sacrifice three times. This made 12 barrels of water poured over the sacrifice. After Elijah had prayed unto God, it is said, "Then the fire of the Lord fell, and consumed the *burnt sacrifice*, and the *wood*, and the *stones*, and the *dust*, and *licked up* the water that was in the trench." (Verse 38) Add five to 12, the number of barrels of water, and the sum is 17, for victory, which was Elijah's that day.

The expression "The dead", is found 14 times in I Corinthians 15 and is connected with the resurrection from the dead. It is found in verses 12, 13, 15, 16, 20, 21, three times in 29, 32, 35, 42, and 52. The word "death" is found five times in this chapter: verses 21, 26, 54, 55, and 56. In verses 51-53, it is said, "Behold, I shew you a mystery; We shall not all sleep, but we shall all be changed, In a moment, in a twinkling of an eye, at the last trump: for the trumpet shall sound and the dead shall be raised incorruptible, and we shall be changed. For this corruptible must put on incorruption, and this mortal must put on immortality." The expression "the dead" is found the 14th time and it's followed by the word "death" which occurs three times; then come the words "victory through our Lord Jesus Christ." The number for salvation is 14, salvation through Jesus Christ. The number for resurrection is three and the resurrection comes through Jesus. When 14, salvation of the body, and three, resurrection, are added they equal 17, for the victory through Jesus. The word "death" occurs five times in the whole chapter, and five represents grace. It will be through the grace of God that the saved dead will rise. Resurrection is discussed throughout this chapter. Add three to five, the number of times death is mentioned, and the total is eight, the new birth. The resurrection of Jesus and those who possess new birth are saved through Him. Only those born again will have victory through Jesus.

Seventeen Greek words are found in I John 5:5, "Who is he that overcometh the world, but he that believeth that Jesus is the Son of God?" In I John 5:4 we read, "and this is the victory." This statement has five Greek words and 17

Greek letters. Here is the quotation in Greek: "KAI ESTIN A VIKA." The second and fourth words have a rough reading which affect the pronunciation of the word but do not interfere with the number of letters. (Here again is five, for grace, and 17, for victory, preceded by 17 Greek words.) Seventeen Greek words are found in this statement: "These shall make war with the Lamb, and the Lamb shall overcome them: for he is Lord of lords, and King of kings:" (Revelation 17:14)

Examples from the Greek language could be multiplied to work out like this, "and this is the victory that overcometh the world, even our faith." (I John 5:4) In his quotation 12 Greek words are found. The 12 Greek words show the divine power through which the believer overcomes the world. The first part of the quotation is, "And this is the victory" that comes through grace and the power of God. Seventeen Greek words follow in the rest of the scripture. The combination of the two statements produce grace, divine power and victory.

Bondage or Binding
"EIGHTEEN"

Eighteen is the number for bondage or binding. In Luke 13:16, Jesus said, "And ought not this woman, being a daughter of Abraham, whom Satan hath bound, lo, these eighteen years, be loosed from this bond of the sabbath day?" The woman was loosed on the Sabbath, or seventh day. When seven is added to 18, they total 25, which represents forgiveness of sins. After we're loosed from Satan's bondage our sins are forgiven us forever. Seven stands for completeness; when Jesus heals, He completely heals. When God forgives our sins, they are completely forgiven. "And you, being dead in your sins and the uncircumcision of your flesh, hath he quickened together with him, having forgiven you all trespasses;" (Colossians 2:13)

In Luke 13, where the woman was healed after being bound for 18 years, we also read about 18 sinners. "the tower of Siloam fell, and slew them, think ye that they were sinners above all men that dwelt in Jerusalem?" (Luke 13:4) Jesus said, "Whosoever committeth sin is the servant of sin." (John 8:34)

In Judges 3:13-14, it is found that Israel was smote by the children of Ammon and Amalek, "and possessed the city of Palm trees. So the children of Israel served Eglon the king of Moab eighteen years."

I wouldn't print an untruth. I do all things in the name of Jesus, the one Lord, Jesus Christ of Nazareth, the power of the Holy Ghost, the one God, the Lord and Saviour Jesus Christ, Who is the Father and stands in judgment over all mankind. This is God's Word, these are God's numbers and they're put together in exactness.

In Judges 10:7-8, the children of Israel are found again in bondage for 18 years, "And the anger of the Lord was hot against Israel, and He sold them into the hands of the Philistines, and in the hands of the children of Ammon. And that year they vexed and oppressed the children of Israel eighteen years, all the children of Israel that were on the other side Jordan in the land of the Amorites, which is in Giland."

There are 18 references to Israel's Egyptian bondage in the Old Testament. They are Genesis 15:13-14; Exodus 1:14; twice in Exodus 2:23; Exodus 6:5; Exodus 6:9; Exodus 13:3; Exodus 13:14; Exodus 20:2; Deuteronomy 5:6; Deuteronomy 6:12, 8:14, 13:5, 13:10 and 26:6; Joshua 24:17; and Judges 6:8.

The tenth time Israel's Egyptian bondage is mentioned is in the verse before the beginning of the Ten Commandments. The law is called "the yoke of bondage." (Galatians 5:1) The first word of the Ten Commandments follows the word "bondage," "I am the Lord thy God, which have brought thee out of the land of Egypt, out of the house of bondage. Thou shalt have no other gods before me." (Exodus 20:2-3) How did it happen that the last word in the ten references to

Israel's bondage came just before the first word of the Ten Commandments? This happened because God wanted it to! This shows His exactness; His perfection of the word which He brought forth.

In Revelation 20:2 there are 18 Greek words, "And he laid hold on the dragon, that old serpent, which is the Devil, and Satan, and bound him a thousand years," In Acts 21:13 Paul said, "for I am ready not to be bound only, but also to die at Jerusalem for the name of the Lord Jesus." Again 18 Greek words. In the 11th verse, the prophet Agabus had taken Paul's Girdle and bound his "hands" and "feet" to picture the binding of Paul at Jerusalem at the hands and feet. In verse 11 there are 18 Greek words.

The Bible has hundreds of pages, yet the number system fits perfectly from beginning to end. Let's proceed to 19.

Faith
"NINETEEN"

Ephesians 2:8 says, "For by grace are ye saved through faith;" Faith is number 19. Five is the number for grace and 14 is the number for salvation. Faith puts us into grace, "By whom also we have access by faith into this grace wherein we stand," (Romans 5:2) At the same time that faith gives us access into grace, it also brings salvation. So when five, for grace, is added to 14, for salvation, the sum is 19, or faith.

There are 38 Greek letters in the statement, "For by grace are ye saved through faith." Add five, for grace, 14, for salvation, 19, for faith, and they total 38, the number of Greek letters found in this statement. We'll look into this statement in another number.

In Paul's discussion of justification by faith in Romans 3:21-5:2, the word "faith" is used 19 times. They are Romans 3:22, 3:25, 3:27, 3:28, 3:30, twice in 3:31, 4:5, 4:9,

4:11, 4:12, 4:13, 4:14, twice in 4:16, 4:19, 4:20, 5:1 and 5:2. Add all the numbers from one to 19 and the total is 190.

In the 11th chapter of Hebrews there are 19 references to salvation through faith.

In Hebrews 11:11 we are told that through faith Sara received strength to conceive and was delivered of a child when she had passed age. The numbers one through 19 equal 190. In an earlier part of this book the combined ages of Sarah and Abraham at the birth of Isaac was 190. (Genesis 17:1-24, 21:5) The difference between the circumcision of Ishmael and Isaac was 13 minus eight, or five, which is the number for grace. There were 14 years difference in the birth of Ishmael and Isaac, which is the number for salvation. The sum of five and 14 is 19, which stands for faith. These three numbers, five, 14 and 19 add up to 38. When 190, the combined ages of Abraham and Sarah at Isaac's birth, is divided by five, for grace, we again get 38. The numbers five, for grace, eight, for the new birth, 14, for salvation, and 19, for faith, are all connected with Isaac. So are 33 and 100, which stand for promise and election, which we'll study later.

Ishmael was born 11 years after Abraham came into Canaan. (Genesis 12:4; 16:16) Eleven is the number for judgment, and flesh is under judgment. Nineteen, faith, connected with the birth of Isaac, a child of promise, and a believer shall not come into judgment. (John 5:24)

This statement in Galatians 3:25-26 has 19 Greek words: "But after that faith is come, we are no longer under a schoolmaster. For ye are all the children of God by faith in Christ Jesus."

The words, "For with the heart man believeth" in Romans 10:10 have 19 Greek letters. The words, "and so ye believed." (I Corinthians 15:11) also have 19 Greek letters. These are only a few of the many examples that show 19 to stand for faith. Using 19 and 36, which stands for enemy, David went out to meet Goliath, the giant who was the enemy of Israel. He went out with faith. He said to Saul, "The Lord that delivered me out of the paw of the lion, and out of the paw of the bear, he will deliver me out of the hand of this Philistine." (I Samuel 17:37) David went out to overcome, or win the victory through faith in God. When 19, faith, is subtracted from 36, enemy, the remainder is 17, or victory. "this is the victory that overcometh the world, even our faith." (I John 5:4) We have already seen that five, for the stones David took up, and 12, for divine authority in which he went out to meet the giant, add up to 17, or victory. Two different combinations shown through the Bible numbers makes the number 17 to be the number for David's victory.

Redemption
"TWENTY"

Twenty is the Bible number for redemption. They made the children of Israel ransom redemption money at the age of 20 years, "When thou taketh the sum of the children of Israel after their number, then shall they give every man a ransom for his soul unto the Lord, when thou numberest them; that there be no plague among them, when thou numberest them. This they shall give, every one that passeth among them that are numbered, half a shekel after the shekel of the sanctuary: (a shekel is twenty gerahs:) an half shekel shall be the offering of the Lord. Every one that passeth among them that are numbered, from twenty years old and above, shall give an offering unto the Lord." (Exodus 30:12-14)

Number 20 was used two times in reference to the redemption money. It was also used twice in reference to the boards of the tabernacle which were set in the sockets made out of silver money paid in redemption for those who were 20 years or older. What they did with the redemption is in Exodus 38:25-28, "And the silver of them that were numbered of the congregation was an hundred talents, and a thousand seven hundred and threescore and fifteen shekels, after the shekel of the sanctuary: A bekah for every man, that is, half a shekel of the sanctuary, for every one that went to be numbered, from twenty years old and upward, for six hundred thousand and three thousand and five thousand and fifty men. And of the hundred talents of silver were cast the sockets of the sanctuary, and the sockets of the vail; an hundred sockets of the hundred talents, a talent for a socket. And of the thousand seven hundred seventy five shekels he made hooks for the pillars, and overlaid their chapiters, and filleted them."

The long side of the tabernacle had 20 boards each, "And thou shalt make the boards for the tabernacle, twenty boards on the south side southward. And thou shalt make forty sockets of silver under the twenty boards; two sockets under one board for his two tenons, and two sockets under another board for his two tenons. And for the second side of the tabernacle on the north side there shall be twenty boards:" (Exodus 26:18-20) The tenons of these boards were set in sockets of silver. The sockets were made of the redemption money. The 20 boards will be considered with number 30.

The 20th time the name of Abram occurs, it is connected with silver, "And Abram was very rich in cattle, in silver, and in gold." (Genesis 13:2) In this place Abram's name is found the 20th time, and it is connected with three things. Three is the number for resurrection, and 20 for redemption. The redemption of our bodies will take place in the resurrection. In this place silver, the metal used in redemption, is also found.

In Ruth 4:1-10, Boaz redeemed the property of Elimeclech, Chilion and Mahlon, purchased Ruth, the widow of Mahlon, to be his wife. The name of Boaz is found 20 times in the book of Ruth. They are 2:1, 2:3, 2:4, 2:5, 2:8, 2:11, 2:15, 2:19, 2:23, 3:2, 3:7, twice in 4:1, 4:5, 4:8, 4:9, 10, 4:13, and twice in 4:21.

Ruth 4:10 is the place the name of Boaz occurs the 17th time. Jesus was crucified on the 14th day of the month and arose from the dead on the 17th day. The raising of the name

90

of the dead is referenced with the name of Boaz the 17th time, "And Boaz said unto the elders, and unto all the people, Ye are witnesses this day, that I have bought all that was Elimelech's, and all that was Chilion's and Mahlon's, of the hand of Naomi. Moreover Ruth the Moabitess, the wife of Mahlon, have I purchased to be my wife, to raise up the name of the dead upon his inheritance," Boaz was the redeemer of that which belonged to the three dead men, Elimelech, Chilion and Mahlon. Now add three, resurrection, and the number 17 and they equal 20, redemption, the number of times the name Boaz appears in the whole book of Ruth. Boaz was also the 20th generation from Shem. The generations are (1) Shem — Genesis 10:10, (2) Arphaxad — Genesis 10:10, (3) Solah — Genesis 10:12, (4) Eber — Genesis 10:14, (5) Peleg — Genesis 10:16, (6) Reu — Genesis 10:18, (7) Serug — Genesis 10:20, (8) Nahor — Genesis 10:22, (9) Terah — Genesis 10:24, (10) Abram — Genesis 10:27, (11) Isaac — Genesis 21:5, (12) Jacob — Genesis 25:24-26, (13) Judah — Genesis 29:35, (14) Phares — Ruth 4:12, (15) Hezron — Ruth 4:18, (16) Ram — Ruth 4:19, (17) Amminadad — Ruth 4:19, (18) Nahshon — Ruth 4:20, (19) Salmon— Ruth 4:21, (20) Boaz — Ruth 4:21.

There are 20 names associated with the house of Israel in the book of Ruth: (1) Elimelech, (2) Naomi, (3) Chilion, (4) Mahlon, (5) Ruth, (6) Boaz, (7) Rachel, (8) Leah, (9) Israel, (10) Judah, (11) Tamar, (12) Tharez, (13) Hezron, (14) Ram, (15) Amminadad, (16) Nahshon, (17) Salmon, (18) Obed, (19) Jesse, (20) David.

The south and north sides of the court of the tabernacle have 20 pillars with 20 silver hooks and each pillar filleted with silver of the redemption money, as in Exodus 27:9-11. The words "we have redemption" in Colossians 1:14 have 20 Greek letters.

The redemption of the believers' bodies will take place as stated, "And not only they, but (1) ourselves also, which have the firstfruits of the Spirit, even we (2) ourselves groan within (3) ourselves, waiting for the adoption, to wit, the redemption of our body." (Romans 8:23)

The words "This is the first resurrection." have 20 Greek letters. The statement "Blessed and holy is he that hath part in the first resurrection: on such the second death hath no power," has 20 Greek words. (Revelation 20:5-6)

Exceeding Sinfulness of Sin "TWENTY-ONE"

Twenty-one is the number that signifies exceeding sinfulness of sin. The 21 sins that are recorded against Israel from Egypt to Jordan are listed and discussed in number 13. Thirteen, associated with sin and rebellion, divided into 273 (Numbers 3:46-48) equals 21, the number of the sins recorded against Israel from Egypt to Jordan. Number 13 indicates the sinful nature as well as the act itself. The outward acts of disobedience were expressions of sinful nature. The sinful nature of man which leads to sin makes redemption necessary through grace. This is why 273 were redeemed with five shekels, and 13 divides into 273 21 times.

After studying the original Greek expression, "exceeding sinful." in Romans 7:13, I found exactly 21 Greek letters.

Paul lists 21 things in II Timothy 3:1-5 about the wickedness of the last days, "This know ye also, that in the last days perilous times shall come. For (1) men shall be lovers of their own selves, (2) coveteous, (3) boasters, (4) proud, (5) blasphemers, (6) disobedient to parents, (7) unthankful, (8) unholy, (9) Without natural affection, (10) trucebreakers, (11) false accusers, (12) incontinent, (13) fierce, (14) despisers of those that do good, (15) Traitors, (16) heady, (17) highminded, (18) lovers of pleasure (19) more than lovers of God; (20) Having a form of godliness, but (21) denying the power thereof: from such turn away."

92

Light/Making Manifest
"TWENTY-TWO"

Twenty-two is the number for light or making manifest. Ephesians 5:13 states, "whatsoever doth make manifest is light." Jesus said, "For every one that doeth evil hateth the light, neither cometh to the light, lest his deeds should be reproved. But he that doeth truth cometh to the light, that his deeds may be made manifest that they are wrought in God." (John 3:20-21)

There were 22 bowls to hold oil for the seven lamps or candlesticks in the tabernacle. There were three branches on each side of the shaft, with three bowls to the branch. This would be six branches, with three bowls to the branch, making 18 on the branches. With 18 bowls in the candlestick itself and the shaft having four bowls, that makes 22 bowls in all. "And thou shalt make a candlestick of pure gold: of beaten work shall the candlestick be made: his shaft, and his branches, his bowls, his knops, and his flowers, shall be the same. And six branches shall come out of the sides of it; three branches of the candlestick out of one side, and three branches of the candlestick out of the other side: Three bowls made like unto almonds, with a knop and a flower in one branch; and three bowls made like almonds in the other branch, with a knop and a flower: so in the six branches that come out of the candlestick. And in the candlestick shall be four bowls made like unto almonds, with their knops and their flowers." (Exodus 25:31-34) This would be three times six or 18 bowls in the six branches. "And in the candlestick shall be four bowls made like unto almonds," This would make 18 bowls in the branches and four in the candlestick or 22 total. The 22 bowls held the oil for the lights.

"Ye are the children of light," (I Thessalonians 5:5) When 14, salvation, is added to eight, new birth, they total 22, for the children of light.

In Acts 22:4-11, Paul was relating what had happened on

the road to Damascus. He said that suddenly a great light shown round about him and he heard a voice saying unto him, Saul, Saul, why persecutest thou me? Saul's name occurs the 21st and the 22nd times in the book of Acts. We find Paul speaking of the great light, and here it is that Saul became a child of the light. "that his deeds may be manifest," (John 3:21) This statement has 22 Greek letters and connects the word "manifest" with 22. The Word of God states, "whatsoever doth make manifest is light." (Ephesians 5:13)

Death
"TWENTY-THREE"

More evidence can be found on the number 23, death, than any other number except resurrection, which will bring God's children out of the second death.

The passage that opened the understanding of death is in Romans 1:28-32, "And even as they did not like to retain God in their knowledge, God gave them over to a reprobate mind, to do those things which are not convenient; (1) Being filled with all unrighteousness, (2) fornication, (3) wickedness, (4) covetousness, (5) maliciousness; (6) full of envy, (7) murder, (8) debate, (9) deceit, (10) malignity; (11) whisperers, (12) Backbiters, (13) haters of God, (14) despiteful, (15) proud, (16) boasters, (17) inventors of evil things, (18) disobedient to parents, (19) Without understanding, (20) covenant breakers, (21) without natural affection, (22) implacable, (23) unmerciful: Who knowing the judgment of God, that they which commit such things are worthy of death, not only do the same, but have pleasure in them that do them."

There are 23 inconvenient things listed above, and, of course, they came from Paul, who followed them by saying,

"Who knowing the judgment of God, that they which commit such things are worthy of death, not only do the same, but have pleasure in them that do them." (Romans 1:28-32)

"Being filled with all unrighteousness," has 23 Greek letters. In the last part of the scripture where the statement "judgment of God," is found, they had brought judgment upon themselves which resulted in death. Numbers 11, judgment, and 12, divine authority, added together equal 23, or death. I Corinthians 15:56 states, "The sting of death is sin; and the strength of sin is the law." Sin and law together result in death.

Paul said, "I was alive without the law once: but when the commandment came, sin revived and I died." (Romans 7:9) Sin alone did not bring death; the law combined to bring death. The law had to be added to ten and 13, representing his sin before death came to him.

All men are born with the sinful nature. Paul stated in Romans, "all have sinned, and come short of the glory of God;" (Romans 3:23) Without new birth, we all will die.

In Numbers 15:32-36, a man brought judgment upon himself by breaking the fourth commandment concerning the Sabbath, the seventh day. That judgment was pronounced by God, "And the Lord said unto Moses, The man shall be surely put to death:" (Verse 35) When 12, divine authority, is added to 11, judgment, the sum is 23, or death.

Genesis 6:12-13 reads, "And God looked upon the earth, and behold, it was corrupt; for all flesh had corrupted his way upon the earth. And God said unto Noah, The end of all flesh is come before me; for the earth is filled with violence through them; and, behold, I will destroy them with the earth." Here the name of Noah appears the tenth time. Man's sin, represented by 13, is seen in this passage. Add ten and 13 and they total 23, death, which came upon all flesh. The 23rd time Noah's name occurs in Genesis 7:23, it is said, "and Noah only remained alive, and they that were with him in the ark." This connects the flood and those who died with 23, death, in two different places.

Noah was of the tenth generation. It was in his day that death was sent upon the ungodly for their sins. Thirteen added to ten equals 23, or death.

Noah's sons, Shem, Ham and Japheth, were of the 11th generation. The number 11, judgment, came in their day. That judgment was executed with divine power and authority. When the number for divine power and authority, 12, is added to 11, judgment, the sum is again 23, or death. So four different times 23 represented death and was connected with the flood.

The account of the destruction of Sodom and Gomorrah is also represented by 23, or death, "And Abraham gat up early in the morning to the place where he stood before the Lord: And he looked toward Sodom and Gomorrah, and toward all the land of the plain, and behold, and, lo, the smoke of the country went up as the smoke of a furnace." (Genesis 19:27-28) The count on the name Abraham comes in Genesis 17:9, not in Genesis 17:5, where he is called Abram.

The number 23 is also associated with the death of Abraham. "Then Abraham gave up the ghost, and died in a good old age, an old man, and full of years; and was gathered to his people. And his sons Isaac and Ishmael buried him in the cave of Machpelah, in the field of Ephron the son of Zohar the Hittite, which is before Mamre." (Genesis 25:8-9) Isaac's name occurs the 23rd time in this account.

A threat of death is found when Jacob's name occurs the 23rd time, "And these words of Esau her elder son were told to Rebekah: and she sent and called Jacob her younger son, and said unto him, Behold, thy brother Esau, as touching thee, doth comfort himself, purposing to kill thee," (Genesis 27:42) The name Jacob occurred the 23rd time in this scripture.

The 23rd time the name of Haman occurs in the book of Esther, the instrument of death fell on Mordecai, "And the thing pleased Haman; and he caused the gallows to be made." (Esther 5:14) Haman's name appears the 23rd time in Esther 5:14. The ten sons of Haman were put to death on the 13th day of the month. (Esther 9:1-10) Numbers ten and 13 added together equal 23, again the number for death. It is law, number ten, and sin, number 13, which bring death. (I Corinthians 15:56)

The evil report of the ten unfaithful spies caused Israel to refuse to go up and possess the land of Canaan. (Numbers 13:25-32) They were turned back into the wilderness until all who had been numbered should die, except Calab and Joshua. When ten, the number of unbelieving spies, is added to 13, the number of Israel's sin, the sum is 23, or death. The ten unfaithful spies represent the law which provoked sin. God said unto those who followed after the ten unfaithful spies, "Doubtless ye shall not come into the land, concerning which I sware to make you dwell therein, save Calab and the son Jephunneh, and Joshua the son of Nun." (Numbers 14:30) The inheritance did not come through the law, represented by the ten unfaithful spies. "For if they which are of the law be heirs, faith is made void, and the promise made of none effect:" (Romans 4:14)

Christ died at the ninth hour of the 14th day. We know that Christ died on the Passover day, or the 14th day of the month. "and there was darkness over all the earth until the ninth hour. And the sun was darkened, and the veil of the temple was rent in the midst. And when Jesus had cried with a loud voice, he said, Father, into thy hands I commend my spirit: and having said thus, he gave up the ghost." (Luke 23:44-46) Matthew connects the tearing of the veil in the temple with Jesus yielding up His Spirit in Matthew 27:50-51. When nine, the hour of death, is added to 14, the sum is 23, or death.

The death of Dorcas, also called Tabitha, came right after Peter's name was mentioned the 23rd time in Acts 9:34. In Acts 9:36-37 the record of the death of Dorcas is given, Peter's name occurs three times, and Dorcas is raised back to life. (Acts 9:36-40) In this instance 23 is death and three, resurrection.

The words "death," "die," "dead" and "dieth" are found

23 times in the book of Hebrews. Dead is found in the same verse where the word "blood" is found the 20th time, "Now the God of peace, that brought again from the dead our Lord Jesus, that great shepard of the sheep, through the blood of the everlasting covenant, Make you perfect in every good work to do his will, working in you that which is wellpleasing in his sight, through Jesus Christ; to whom be glory for ever and ever. Amen." (Hebrews 13:20-21) The book deals with redemption from death. Number 20 stands for redemption, and redemption comes through the blood. In the same verse, death comes under consideration the 23rd time, and the blood which redeems occurs the 20th time.

Number 23 is found three times in Revelation 17:3, "So he carried me away in the spirit into the wilderness: and I saw a woman sit upon a scarlet coloured beast, full of names of blasphemy, having seven heads and ten horns." The word "beast" occurs the 23rd time in this scripture. There are also 23 Greek words in that statement. A woman, the great harlot, is mentioned six times in verses 3, 4, 6, 7, 9, and 18, and is seen on a beast with seven heads and ten horns. When six, seven and ten are added together the total is 23, death. John was told in Revelation 17:2-3 that he would be shown the judgment of the great whore. In verse 18, John said, "And the woman which thou sawest is the great city, which reigneth over the kings of the earth." In Revelation 18:8, John states, "Therefore shall her plagues come in one day, death, and mourning, and famine; and she shall be utterly burned with fire: for strong is the Lord God who judgeth her." Here the word "death" is found, and the judgment of God is also mentioned. When 11, judgment, is added to 12, divine authority, they equal 23, or death upon the woman or city. Number 23 is mentioned four times concerning the death of the woman harlot. The beast is mentioned the 23rd time in Revelation 17:3. There are 23 words in the statement of that verse. The seven heads and ten horns of the beast and number six, connected with the woman, add up to 23, or death.

In Revelation 20:12, John said, "And I saw the dead, small and great, stand before God; and the books were opened:" This is the 23rd time the word "open" is found in Revelation, and the word "death" is found in this verse.

In I John 5:16 the statement is made, "There is a sin unto death: I do not say that he shall pray for it." In this statement there are ten Greek words. The word "sin" is found in the statement, and the number 13 stands for sin. Add number 13, or sin, to ten, the number of Greek words in the statement, and they total 23, or death. In the words, "There is a sin unto death:" there are 23 Greek letters.

In I John 3:14, John states, "We know that we have passed from death unto life, because we love the brethren. He that loveth not his brother abideth in death." There are 23 words in the whole verse, and the 23rd word is death. If the count is stopped with "because we love the brethren." the count would only be 14 words, and 14 is the number for salvation.

When three, resurrection, is subtracted from 23, death, it leaves 20, or the redemption of the body. The resurrection of God's children will bring redemption of their bodies and death never again.

The statement about the two witnesses being killed in Revelation 11:7 has 23 Greek words. The statement about the seven thousand being killed in an earthquake in Revelation 11:13 has 23 words. In Luke 23:33, we read, "And when they were come to the place, which is called Calvary, there they crucified him, and the malfactors, one on the right hand and the other on the left." Again this has 23 Greek words.

When Lazarus died, they bound his hands and his feet with grave cloths and covered his face with a napkin. In the Greek, the divine article "the" is used with the hands, feet and face. *When this divine article is left out of the translation — the feet, the hands and the face — there are 23 Greek letters.*

There are nearly 50 examples, such as above, that can be explained where 23 is connected with death.

Let's take Paul's voyage toward Rome. In Acts 27:20-24

there is the account of the storm and the shipwreck. Acts 27:37 states that there were 276 on that ship. They faced death in the storm. The 20th verse states that "all hope that we should be saved was then taken away." Then God sent His angel to tell Paul that there would be no loss of life. Upon the authority of God's Word, Paul told them that none would die. When 276, the number of men on the ship, is divided by 12, for the divine authority, it comes out exactly 23 times, or the number for death. The numbers from one to 23 added together equal 276, the number on the ship that faced death. They were saved on the 14th day, and 14 is the number for salvation. (Please read verses 33-44.)

Twenty-three, or death, has been covered from Genesis to Revelation. It has been connected over and over again with death in the account of the flood. Jesus told me this: that it was in the beginning of the foundation and even before the world began. This numbering system was in the mind of God at the time of the flood and even before the world began. It was connected with the number (276) who were on the ship on which Paul sailed. It has been seen that they were saved from the storm and the sea on the 14th day. God connects this number with salvation in Genesis and Exodus. Had there been 277 on that ship the numbers would not have been divisible by 23 and 12. Had there been just 275 men on the ship, the division would not be even either. Had they landed on an island on the 13th day or any other day that wouldn't have connected the 14 for salvation. God could not have fixed His number system to fit perfectly with the numbers connected with the ship and storm unless He had foreknown all of these things. He had to foresee all things, to see that exactly 276 men, no more and no less, boarded that ship. He had to control the drift of the ship, the wind and the waves to cause the men to be saved on the 14th day. Who can study these things and then limit the power of the foreknowledge of God, of Jesus Christ? Every line, every scripture, every word, every letter used had to be in the mind of God when He created this numbering system. Jesus said, "Heaven and

earth shall pass away, but my words shall not pass away."
(Matthew 24:35) What is the wisdom and power of man in
comparison with all this? Jesus asked me this question. It is
the most wonderful thing within my mind!

Priesthood
"TWENTY-FOUR"

Twenty-four is the number connected with the priesthood.
In I Chronicles 24:1-9, the 24 divisions of the priesthood are
found. Each group had a chief man as its head. There were 16
chief men of the house of Eleazar, and eight of the house of
Ithamar. (Verses 1-4) Eight represents the new birth and 16
represents love. A believer priest had to be born again with
love in his heart if he truly interceded for others. There are
24 hours in a day; sinful man is interceded for every hour of
the day and night. Aaron wore the breastplate upon his heart,
the seat of love or affection. (Exodus 28:29) The number 23
stands for death. In I John 5:16, John said, "If any man see
his brother sin a sin which is not unto death, he shall ask, and
he shall give him life for them that sin not unto death." Inter-
cession, death and life are all related.

In Revelation 4:4, John saw 24 elders sitting on 24 seats.
In Revelation 5:8-10 he heard them singing that Christ had
redeemed them by His blood and had made them kings and
priests unto God and Christ Jesus.

Forgiveness of Sins
"TWENTY-FIVE"

Twenty-five stands for the forgiveness of sins. Jehoiachin,
king of Judah, was pardoned from prison on the 25th day of

the month, "And it came to pass in the seven and thirtieth year of the captivity of Jehoiachin king of Judah, in the twelfth month, in the five and twentieth day of the month, that Evil Merodach, king of Babylon in the first year of his reign lifted up the head of Jehoiachin king of Judah, and brought him forth out of prison, And spake kindly unto him, and set his throne above the throne of the kings that were with him in Babylon, And changed his prison garments: and he did continually eat bread before him all the days of his life." (Jeremiah 52:31-33) King Jehoiachin was a pardoned sinner. When God forgives a man of his sins, He deals kindly with him. He takes away his garments of unrighteousness and clothes him in the righteousness which God Himself provides. God provides for us all the days of our life.

King Jehoiachin was pardoned on the 25th day of the 12th month. Here we see number 12, divine authority and power by which man must be forgiven of his sins, and 25, which stands for forgiveness of sins. Please notice how the numbers word together. This took place in the 37th year of Jehoiachin's capacity, the 12th month, on the 25th day. Numbers 12 and 25 add up to 37, the first number found in the statement. Notice how all this connects with Mark 2:7, "who can forgive sins but God only?" In the words "who can forgive sins" there are 25 Greek letters, and in "but God only" there are 12 Greek letters. We find the number 25, forgiveness of sins, and number 12, divine authority, by which sins are forgiven. Altogether there are 37 letters. Here are the numbers which were found in Jeremiah 52:31-33, in connection with Jehoiachin's pardon: 37, 12 and 25. Number 25 is the number five, for grace, plus 20, for redemption, which is 13, for sin, plus 12, for divine authority, by which man's sins are forgiven.

Gospel
"TWENTY-SIX"

"Moreover, brethren, I declare unto you the gospel which I preached unto you, which also ye have received, and wherein ye stand; By which also ye are saved, if ye keep in memory what I preached unto you, unless ye have believed in vain. For I delivered unto you first of all that which I also received, how that Christ *died* for our sins according to the scriptures; And that he was buried, and that he *rose again* the *third* day according to the scriptures:" (I Corinthians 15:1-4) The gospel is the good news of the resurrection of Jesus Christ. In addition to the good news of His death for our sins, it takes both the death and resurrection of Jesus to accomplish the good news. When three, for the resurrection, is added to 23, for death, then the sum is 26, for the gospel.

Dorcas, or Tabitha, died just after Peter's name occurred in Acts 9:34-37. Then Peter's name occurs three more times: verses 38, 39, and 40; and he raised Dorcas back to life again. So the death of Dorcas took place following the 23rd mention of Peter; then she was raised up again when Peter's name was mentioned the 26th time. This was good news to the disciples.

Proclamation of the Gospel and Prophecy
"TWENTY-SEVEN"

Twenty-seven is a number that is somewhat difficult to determine. What Jesus did give connects this number with the proclaiming of the gospel and also with prophecy. There is an element of prophecy in the preaching of the gospel. Prophecy foretells the future resurrection and the glorification of the saints of God. As Jesus arose from the dead, so shall the saints of God arise.

The 27th time Peter's name occurs in the book of Acts is where he presented Dorcas alive to the disciples, "But Peter put them all forth, and kneeled down, and prayed; and turning him to the body said, Tabitha, arise. And she opened her eyes: and when she saw Peter, she sat up. And he gave her his hand, and lifted her up, and when he had called the saints and widows, presented her alive." (Acts 9:40-41) Peter's name occurs the 26th time when he prayed and told Tabitha to arise. She then opens her eyes, and his name occurs the 27th time when he presents her alive to the people.

After Jesus was crucified for our sins He arose again, then the message of the same was proclaimed in Romans 1:15 and 16, "So, as much as in me is, I am ready to preach the gospel to you that are at Rome also. For I am not ashamed of the gospel of Christ: for it is the power of God unto salvation to every one that believeth;" This has 27 Greek words. Paul said to the elders of the church in Ephesians (Acts 20:28), "Take heed therefore unto yourselves, and to all the flock, over the which the Holy Ghost hath made you overseers, to feed the church of God, which he hath purchased with his own blood." This passage also has 27 Greek words.

In Galatians 2:1-2, Paul said, "Then fourteen years after I went up again to Jerusalem with Barnabas, and took Titus with me also. And I went up by revelation, and communicated unto them that gospel which I preach among the Gentiles," There are 27 Greek words in this statement.

In Revelation 13:1, John prophesied of the beast that was to come having seven heads, ten horns and ten crowns, "and upon his heads the name of blasphemy." These numbers, 7, 10 and 10, add up to 27.

From this it seems that number 27 is connected with the preaching of the gospel and prophecy. Perhaps God will reveal more at a later date.

Eternal Life
"TWENTY-EIGHT"

Twenty-eight is the number for eternal life, without a doubt. This was found by a combination of numbers found in certain verses where the words "eternal life" were found. This is found by examining the original Greek verses in various different instances where eternal life is found having 28 words or 28 Greek letters. "But where sin abounded, grace did much more abound: That as sin hath reigned unto death, [23] even so might grace [five] reign through righteousness unto eternal life by Jesus Christ our Lord." (Romans 5:20-21) When five, grace, is added to 23, death, the total is 28, or eternal life.

In John 5:24 there are five positive statements, and the last statement is, "but is passed from death unto life." "(1) He that heareth my word, (2) and believeth on him that sent me, (3) hath everlasting life, (4) and shall not come into condemnation; (5) but is passed from death [number 23] unto life." There are five verbs found in this verse. They are (1) heareth, (2) believeth, (3) hath, (4) shall not come, and (5) is passed. In the five divisions of this statement grace is found. In the fifth and last division it is said, "but is passed from death unto life." Grace took us out of death and passed us over into the realm of eternal or everlasting life. When five, grace, is added to 23, death, the sum is 28, or eternal life.

Romans 6:23 states, "For the wages of sin is death; but the gift of God is eternal life through Jesus Christ our Lord." The statement, "but the gift of God is eternal life" has 28 Greek letters and seven words. When the numbers from one to seven are added, the total is 28. The same is found in John 10:27-29 in which there are seven positive statements which are made in the indicative mood — both in English and the original Greek language. According to the rules of English, the indicative mood expresses a positive or undoubted fact. To insert the word "if" into his passage, as is so often done, would change the mood in any passage to subjective. No one has any more right to change the mood in any passage than to change anything else in the Bible. Those seven positive statements are: "(1) My sheep hear my voice, (2) and I know them, (3) and they follow me: (4) And I give unto them eternal life; (5) and they shall never perish, (6) neither shall any man pluck them out of my hand. (7) My Father, which gave them me, is greater than all; and no man is able to pluck them out of my Father's hand." (John 10:27-29) First, they hear the voice of Christ; second, Christ knows them; third, they follow Christ; fourth, Christ gives them eternal life; fifth, they shall never perish; sixth, no one shall pluck them out of the hand of Jesus; and, seventh, none is able to pluck them out of the Father's hand. In the fourth statement, Jesus said, "I give unto them eternal life;" (7 x 4 = 28, or eternal life.) Add the numbers from one to seven in the same statement and the sum is 28, the exact number of Greek letters in the expression, "but the gift of God is eternal life"

Twenty-eight is two times 14, and the number 14 is salvation. Eternal life is given to us for salvation of our soul with a guarantee of salvation of our bodies. Twenty, redemption, plus eight, new birth, equals 28, or eternal life.

The 28th time that Noah's name occurs in Genesis 8:15-16, it states, "And God spake unto Noah, saying, Go forth of the ark, thou, and thy wife, and thy sons, and thy sons' wives with thee." As Noah and his family entered the ark, we picture them passing into eternal life and entering the blessed age to come.

Departure
"TWENTY-NINE"

Twenty-nine is the number for departure. When Jesus raised Lazarus from the dead, He said, "Lazarus, come forth." Then it is said, "And he that was dead came forth, bound hand and foot with graveclothes: and his face was bound about with a napkin. Jesus saith unto them, loose him, and let him go." (John 11:43-44) From the first word Jesus spoke to Lazarus until He said, "let him go" there were 29 Greek words used. The 29th word is "go".

The 29th time the name of Noah is found is where he, and all that were with him, went forth out of the ark. (Genesis 8:18 & 19) The 29th time the name of Abraham occurs is where the kings who had overtook the kings of Sodom and Gomorrah took Lot with his goods and departed. (Genesis 14:12) The 29th time the name Isaac occurs is where he left Laharroi and went unto Abimelech in Gerar. (Genesis 25:11-26:1) The 29th time the name of Jacob is found is in the place where he had left Canaan and had gone to Padanaram. (Genesis 28:7) The 29th time the name of Laban is found is when God told Jacob to leave Laban's place and return to the land of his father. The 29th time the name of Samson occurs is where he awoke out of his sleep and went away with the pin of the beam and web. (Judges 16:14)

Blood
"THIRTY"

Thirty is the number for blood and associated with the blood of Jesus. Judas betrayed Jesus for 30 pieces of silver. "Then Judas, which had betrayed him, when he saw that he was condemned, repented himself, and brought again the thirty pieces of silver to the chief priests and elders, Saying, I have sinned in that I have betrayed the innocent blood." (Matthew 27:3-4)

In Revelation 5:9, the redeemed said of Jesus, "And they sung a new song, saying, Thou art worthy to take the book, and to open the seals thereof: for thou wast slain, and hast redeemed us to God by thy blood out of every kindred, and tongue, and people, and nation;" There are 30 Greek words in this statement. In the statement, "hast redeemed us to God by thy blood" (Revelation 5:9) there are 30 Greek letters. The statement, "being now justified by his blood," (Romans 5:9) has 30 Greek letters.

The 30th time the name of Noah occurs is in Genesis 8:20, "And Noah builded an altar unto the Lord; and took of every clean beast, and of every clean fowl, and offered burnt offerings on the altar." In this passage there can be seen the shedding of blood. This blood was typical of the blood of Jesus.

The 30th time the name of Samuel occurs is found in I Samuel 7:9, "And Samuel took a suckling lamb, and offered it for a burnt offering wholly unto the Lord:" Here again the shedding of blood is seen. The first time the word "blood" is found in the Bible is in Genesis 4:9-10. "And the Lord said unto Cain, Where is Abel thy brother? And he said, I know not: Am I my brother's keeper? And he said, What hast thou done? the voice of thy brother's blood crieth unto me from the ground." Up to this time the name of Adam had occurred 12 times, Eve two times, Cain nine times, and Abel seven times, totaling 30. The 30th mention of a name is that of Abel whose blood was shed. Ironical?

The blood of the lamb of God is spoken of in Revelation 5:6-9: "And I beheld, and, lo, in the midst of the throne and of the four beasts, and in the midst of the elders, stood a Lamb as it had been slain, having seven horns and seven eyes, which are the seven Spirits of God sent forth into all the earth." (Verse 6) John saw the Lamb, which was Jesus, that had been slain and that seven in this verse is the 23rd time the word "seven" is found in the book of Revelation. Here we find 23, death; and when seven is added to 23 that makes 30, for the blood of the Lamb that died.

Then John went on to say, "And when he had taken the book, the four beasts [4] and four and twenty elders [24] fell down before the Lamb, (1) having every one of them harps, and golden vials full of odours, which are the prayers of the saints. And they sung a new song, saying Thou are worthy to take the book, and to open the seals thereof: for thou wast slain, and hast redeemed us to God by thy blood out of every kindred, and tongue, and people, and nation;" Thirty different ones are mentioned and the Lamb that was slain is the 30th. Him on the throne — that's one — and four beasts or living creatures — that's five — the 24 elders — that's 29 — and the Lamb that was slain totals 30, representing the blood of the Lamb.

We have already seen that number 14, salvation and the repentant thief was saved on the 14th day of the month, the day Jesus was crucified. The words of the promise Jesus made to him, "Today shalt thou be with me in paradise." (Luke 23:43) has 30 Greek letters. The law was fulfilled by the blood of Jesus.

Over the linen curtains of the tabernacle there was a cover made of 11 curtains of goats hair, which were 30 cubits long and four cubits wide. Five of these were coupled together, the other six were coupled together and these two broad curtains were fastened together with 50 taches of brass. The group of six were in front with one double in the forefront of the tabernacle. (Exodus 26:7-10) This made the brass taches in the goats hair curtains to come over the vail even as the gold taches in the linen curtains. In the 11 curtains of goats hair we see Jesus bringing out judgment on the cross. With the brass taches of the curtains coming over the vail we see Jesus being lifted up as was the serpent of brass in the wilderness. (Numbers 21:8-9; John 3:14-15) The 30 cubits length of the goats hair curtains represented the blood of Jesus which was shed on the cross where He bore the judgment of sins of the lost world. In the four cubits, the width of the curtains, there is seen the truth that the blood of Jesus was shed to save the lost man from sin. The number 30, blood of Jesus, equals ten, the law, plus 20, or redemption. "when the fulness of the time has come, God sent forth his Son, made of a woman, made under the law, To redeem them that were under the law, that we might receive the adoption of sons."

(Galatians 4:4-5) It took the blood of Christ to redeem from the law. Having seen that 30 stands for the blood of Jesus, and that Jesus redeemed us from the law, let us read Ephesians 1:7 in the light of the Bible numbers. "In whom we have redemption through his blood, the forgiveness of sins, according to the riches of his grace;" Number 20 is for redemption, number ten is for the law, number 30 is for the blood of Jesus, number 25 is for the forgiveness of sins, and number five is for grace. In this verse the results of this redemption is the forgiveness of sins, according to the riches of God's grace. When 25, forgiveness of sins, is added to five, grace, in this verse they equal 30, the blood of Jesus.

The tabernacle was made of boards standing up. (Exodus 26:13) These boards were ten cubits long and a cubit and a half wide. (Exodus 26:16) There were 20 boards in each of the sides, south and north. (Exodus 26:18-20) When the 20 boards are multiplied by a cubit and a half, the width of each board, that makes 30 cubits as the length of the tabernacle. The 20 boards were held together with five bars to the side. (Exodus 26:26-28) The 20 boards and five bars and the 20 boards made 25 pieces of material to the side. In the long side of the tabernacle (1) the number of boards is 20 for redemption, (2) the height was ten cubits for the number for the law, (3) the length was 30 cubits, which stands for the blood of Jesus, (4) 25 pieces of material stands for the forgiveness of sins, (5) five bars is the number for grace. In the long side of the tabernacle there is pictured redemption, 20, the law, ten, the blood of Jesus, 30, forgiveness of sins, 25, or according to the riches of God's grace, number five. Thus all the doctrine in Ephesians 1:7 and in Galatians 4:15 are shown in the numbers in the long side of the tabernacle. Who but God could draw a picture like this?

Under 20, which stands for redemption, it was shown that Boaz redeemed the property of Elimelech, Chilion and Mahlon. (Ruth 4:1-11) It was also proven that the name of Boaz was found 20 times in the book of Ruth and that he was the 20th in the lineage of Shem, the new line that started

110

after the flood. Going back to Adam, Boaz is 30 in line. (See the generations of Shem in Genesis 11:10-26.) This brings in the record of Abraham. To this add the names of Isaac, Jacob and Judah and then take up with Pharez, Judah's son in Ruth 4:18-22. This will show that Boaz was the 20th in the generation from Shem and the 30th from Adam. He was connected with redemption, and redemption is through the blood. Both 20 and 30, the numbers for redemption and blood, are connected with Boaz. He was the 20th from Shem and the 30th from Adam. The numbers never fail to fall in place.

Offspring or Seed
"THIRTY-ONE"

The following are examples of how God used the number 31 in producing offspring or furthering his seed.

Noah's name occurs the 31st time when God said unto him, "Be fruitful, and multiply, and replenish the earth." (Genesis 9:1)

Abram occurs the 31st time where the word speaks of his trained servants born unto his house. (Genesis 14:4)

Abraham's name occurs the 31st time where he prayed for the house of Abimelech, his wife and maidservants so that they might bare children. (Genesis 20:17-18)

The 31st time the name of Jacob occurs is when he had awakened out of his sleep after God had told him his seed would be as the dust of the earth. (Genesis 28:13-16)

There are many more examples, but I hope these will suffice.

Covenant
"THIRTY-TWO"

There are 32 references in the book of Deuteronomy to the Abrahamic covenant. Boaz and Ruth were in the lineage of Jesus, in Whom the covenant with Abraham was confirmed. (Galatians 3:17) The name of Boaz is found 20 times in the book of Ruth, and the name Ruth is found 12 times. When 12 is added to 20, the sum is 32, the number for covenant. The number 12, which stands for divine authority, added to number 20, for redemption, equals 32, for covenant. The 32nd time Noah's name occurs is found where God made a covenant with him, "And God spake unto Noah, and to his sons with him, saying, And I, behold, I establish my covenant with you, and with your seed after you;" (Genesis 9:8-9)

Promise
"THIRTY-THREE"

Thirty-three is the number for promise. In Ephesians 2:12, the expression "covenants of Promise," is found. The word "promise" follows the word covenant.

The 33rd time Noah's name is found is where God gave the rainbow as a sign of His promise to Noah and future generations. (Genesis 9:13-17) Water will not destroy the earth again.

Isaac was a child of promise, "Now we, brethren, as Isaac was, are the children of promise." (Galatians 4:28) Abraham's name occurs the 33rd time when Isaac is born. "And the Lord visited Sarah as he had said, [was this not the promise?] For Sarah conceived, and bare Abraham a son in his old age, at the set time of which God had spoken to him." (Genesis 21:1-2) God fulfilled the promise to Abraham and his name occurs the 33rd time.

In Galatians 4:23 these words are found, "but he of the freewoman was by promise." In the Greek text there are 33 letters and eight Greek words in this statement. This fits perfectly with Genesis 21:1-4. In Genesis 21:4 it is said, "And Abraham circumcised his son Isaac being eight days old," Why are there 33 Greek letters and eight Greek words about Isaac in Galatians 4:23? The number of letters agree with the 33rd time Abraham's name was found, in connection with the birth of Isaac, the child of promise. The eight Greek words agree with the number of days on which Isaac was circumcised!

Endurance
"THIRTY-FOUR"

The number 34 has been difficult to identify. After much study, searching, prayer and fasting, God has revealed it to mean endurance. When God tested the faith of Abraham by asking for Isaac as a sacrifice, his faith endured and he was victorious.

Hope
"THIRTY-FIVE"

Thirty-five is the number connected with hope, "And now abideth faith, hope, and charity, these three; but the greatest of these is charity." (I Corinthians 13:13) When 19, faith, is added to 16, love, they total 35 for hope.

The birth of Enos was mentioned being connected with 105. (Genesis 5:6) When Enos was born men began to call upon the name of the Lord. (Genesis 4:26) Fourteen, or salvation, "whosoever shall call upon the name of the Lord shall be saved." (Romans 10:13) When the numbers from one to 14 are added, the sum is 105, the number connected with the birth of Enos. Enos was the third in the lineage of Adam. When three is multiplied by 35, which stands for the believer's hope, the sum is 105, again connected with the birth of Enos.

Enemy
"THIRTY-SIX"

Thirty-six is the number for enemy. The 36th time the name of Haman occurs is where Esther called him the adversary and enemy. "And Esther said, The adversary and the enemy is this wicked Haman. Then Haman was afraid before the king and the queen." (Esther 7:6) In this place Haman's name occurs the 35th and 36th times. His hope of having the Jews put to death was taken away, as he was set forth as the enemy of the Jews. He was called the Jew's enemy in Esther 3:4. The sixth time his name occurs is in Esther 3:6, where he sought to have all the Jews put to death. This was a violation of the sixth commandment, "Thou shalt not kill." (Exodus 20:13) Six times six is 36. The 36th time the name of Abram occurs is where God said to him, "Fear not, Abram: I am thy shield," (Genesis 15:1) A shield is a protector from the enemy.

The 36th time David's name is found is in I Samuel 17:50, and it is where he overcame his enemy, Goliath, with a sling and a stone. Goliath had the number six in his height. "And there went out a champion out of the camp of the Philistines, named Goliath, of Gath, whose height was six cubits and a span. And he had a helmet of brass upon his head, and he was armed with a coat of mail; and the weight of the coat was five thousand shekels of brass. And he had greaves of brass upon his legs, and a target of brass between his shoulders. And the staff of his spear was like a weaver's beam; and his spear's head weighed six hundred shekels of iron: and one bearing a shield went before him." (I Samuel 17:4) David went out to meet his enemy with his faith fixed in God. David said, "moreover, The Lord that delivered me out of the paw of the lion, and out of the paw of the bear, he will deliver me out of the hand of this Philistine." (I Samuel 17:37) The number for faith is 19, and victory, 17; when you take 19, faith, from 36, enemy, you have the victory or 17. David won his victory through his faith in God.

There are 36 references to the beast in the book of Revelation and the numbers one through 36 add up to 666, the number of the beast. (Revelation 13:18) The beast is referred to in the following places: (1) 11:7, (2) 13:1, (3) 13:2, (4) 13:3, (5, 6 & 7) 13:4, (8 & 9) 13:12, (10 & 11) 13:14, (12, 13 & 14) 13:15, (15) 13:17, (16) 13:18, (17) 14:9, (18) 14:11, (19) 15:2, (20) 16:2, (21) 16:10, (22) 16:13, (23) 17:3, (24) 17:7, (25 & 26) 17:8, (27) 17:11, (28) 17:12, (29) 17:13, (30) 17:16, (31) 17:17, (32) 19:19, (33 & 34) 19:20, (35) 20:4 and (36) 20:10. A total of 36, all in Revelation.

The four beasts are from the word "Zoan." This word is not to be confused with the word "thereon," for the evil beast of Revelation. The beast will be the great enemy of the saints before the great tribulations. (Revelation 13:7) In Revelation 13:2 it states, "And the beast which I saw was like unto a leopard, and his feet were as the feet of a bear, and his mouth as the mouth of a lion: and the dragon gave him his power, and his seat, and great authority." This statement has 36 Greek words. When six, Satan, who is called the dragon, is added to 36, the number of times the beast is mentioned, we get a total of 42; the beast will continue 42 months. "and power was given unto him to continue forty and two months." (Revelation 13:5) The word "dragon" occurs 13 times in Revelation. The numbers one through 13 add up to 91. When 36, the number of times the word "dragon" is found, is added to 42, the number of months the beast will be in power, they equal 91.

As you receive the revelation of the numbers through the power of the Holy Ghost, you'll know that God is Jesus, in the Godhead a Father, Son and Holy Ghost, that which arose in the resurrection, being three — Father, Son and Holy Ghost, the Godhead of one in unity. With three titles to One God, Jesus being His name when manifested in the flesh. Jesus said, "I am come in my Father's name," (John 5:43) Jesus also said, "I and my Father are one." (John 10:30) "he that hath seen me hath seen the Father;" (John 14:9)

Exaltation
"THIRTY-SEVEN"

Thirty-seven is the number for exaltation. David was exalted when he overthrew his enemy. The beast, who is the enemy, is cast into the lake of fire, and the devil, another enemy, is put into the bottomless pit; then the glorified saints of God will be exalted to rule and reign with Jesus 1000 years. (Revelation 19:19, 20:6)

In the 37th year of his imprisonment, the 25th day of the 12th month, Jehoiachin was pardoned from prison, his throne was set above the thrones of the kings that were with him in Babylon, "And it came to pass in the seven and thirtieth year of the captivity of Jehoiachin king of Judah, in the twelfth month, in the five and twentieth day of the month, that evil-Merodack king of Babylon in the first year of his reign lifted up the head of Jehoiachin king of Judah, and brought him forth out of prison, And spake kindly unto him, and set his throne above the throne of the kings that were with him in Babylon," (Jeremiah 52:31 & 32)

Jehoiachin was exalted in the 37th year of his captivity, on the 25th day of the 12th month. These two numbers add up to 37, corresponding with the 37th year. In this scripture are mentioned 12 (divine authority, which pardons and exalts), 25 (for pardon or forgiveness of sins) and 37 (or Exaltation).

Righteousness
"THIRTY-EIGHT"

Thirty-eight seems to be the number that stands for righteousness. It is the sum of five, grace, 14, salvation, and 19, or faith. Romans 3:22-24, righteousness that comes by faith and justification that is by grace. Jesus told me that 38 is righteousness. Righteousness and grace are connected with the reign of the saints. "For if by one man's offense death reigned by one; much more they which receive abundance of grace and of the gift of righteousness shall reign in life by one, Jesus Christ." (Romans 5:17) After the beast, 36, is put down and the saints are exalted, 37, to reign with Jesus, the earth will have righteous rule, "Behold, a king shall reign in righteousness, and princes shall rule in judgment." (Isaiah 32:1)

Truth
"THIRTY-NINE"

Thirty-nine surely seems to stand for truth. After the saints are exalted to reign with Jesus and to rule in righteousness on the earth, then truth will prevail. "They shall not hurt nor destroy in all my holy mountain: for the earth shall be full of the knowledge of the Lord, as the waters cover the sea." (Isaiah 11:9) "Thus saith the Lord; I am returned unto

117

Zion, and will dwell in the midst of Jerusalem: and Jerusalem shall be called a city of truth; and the mountain of the Lord of hosts the holy mountain." (Zechariah 8:3) "but grace and truth came by Jesus Christ." There are 39 Greek letters in John 1:17.

Tribulation or Trial
"FORTY"

Our Lord was tempted 40 days, "And immediately the Spirit driveth him into the wilderness. And he was there in the wilderness forty days, tempted by Satan;" (Mark 1:12 & 13)

Israel was 40 years in the wilderness. "Harden not your hearts, as in the provocation, in the day of the temptation, in the wilderness: When your fathers tempted me, proved me, and saw my works forty years." (Hebrews 3:8 & 9) Israel was tried 40 days when Moses was in the mountain. "and Moses was in the mount forty days and forty nights." (Exodus 24:18) "And when the people saw that Moses delayed to come down out of the mount, the people gathered themselves together unto Aaron, and said unto him, Up, make us gods, which shall go before us; for as for this Moses, the man that brought us up out of the land of Egypt, we wot not what is become of him." (Exodus 32:1)

Four times ten (four and ten are the numbers of the natural man under the law) equals 40. The natural man under the law fall into temptation, as did Israel. Forty is five times eight (the numbers for grace and the new birth). The grace of God, five, enables one with the new birth, eight, to withstand temptation. Forty is 20 for the redemption of the soul, plus 20 for the redemption of the body, which will place God's children above the reach of temptation.

Deception
"FORTY-ONE"

FORTY-ONE is the number for DECEPTION. The serpent tempted Eve and deceived her. "but the woman being deceived was in the transgression." (I Timothy 2:14)

There are 41 Greek words in II Corinthians 11:13-15. "For such are false apostles, deceitful workers, transforming themselves into the apostles of Christ. And no marvel; for Satan himself is transformed into an angel of light. Therefore it is no great thing if his ministers also be transformed as the ministers of righteousness; whose end shall be according to their works."

The next number, 42, stands for the SECOND COMING OF JESUS CHRIST. Just before He returns — especially just before He returns to the earth — there will be a time of great DECEPTION. Please read II Thessalonians 2:7-10, II Timothy 3:1-7, and II Timothy 3:13.

Second Coming of Jesus
"FORTY-TWO"

Let's take 42. Number 42 is the number associated with the Coming of Jesus: both His first coming and the two manifestations at His second advent (He came into the world the first time in the 42nd generation from Abraham). He is coming back for His saints before the 42-month reign of the beast, perhaps 42 months before the beast's reign begins. He will return to the earth at the end of the 42-month reign of the beast to put an end to the wicked reign. The marvelous way in which this number works is the wonder of all wonders. My children of God, the time is at hand!

"So all the generations from Abraham to David are fourteen generations; and from David until the carrying away into Babylon are fourteen generations; and from the carrying away into Babylon unto Christ are fourteen generations." That is in Matthew 1:17. Here are 14 generations three times over. Three times 14 makes 42. Here is the number three for the Resurrection, and 14 for Salvation.

"And she shall bring forth a son, and thou shalt call His name JESUS: for he shall save his people from their sins." See Matthew 1:21. Christ is also the "Resurrection, and the life:" That is in John 11:25. When Jesus comes for His saints, the dead in Christ will be raised and the salvation of their bodies will take place. "and unto them that look for him shall he appear the second time without sin unto salvation." (Hebrews 9:28)

When three for the resurrection is multiplied by 14 for salvation, the product is 42, for the coming of Christ. When Jesus raised Lazarus, He spoke three words, "Lazarus, come forth." That is in John 11:43. There are also three Greek words here which have 14 letters. Here again the number three, for the resurrection, and 14, for salvation or deliverance, follow these three words with 14 letters. Lazarus came forth from the grave. When the three words are added to the 14 letters, they total 17 for victory out of the grave, "O grave, where is thy victory?" (I Corinthians 15:55) "thanks be to God, which giveth us the victory through our (1) Lord (2) Jesus (3) Christ." This is in I Corinthians 15:57.

When the 14 letters in the three words Jesus spoke to Lazarus are multiplied by the three words the product is 42, for the second coming of Jesus. Fourteen times three is 42.

In all of this, there is a picture of what will take place when Jesus comes for His saints. Then the resurrection will take place, and three is for the resurrection. The salvation of their bodies will take place and 14 is the number for salvation. There is victory over death and the grave: three for resurrection and 14 for salvation total 17, the number for victory. "So when this corruptible shall have put on incorruption, and this mortal shall have put on immortality, then shall be brought to pass the saying that is written, Death is swallowed up in victory." (I Corinthians 15:54)

All of this will be brought about at the coming of the Lord Jesus. When three for the resurrection of the bodies is multiplied by 14, the product is 42, for the coming of the Lord Jesus, when all this takes place.

According to the Greek, the word "anastasis" is found 42 times in the New Testament. In the translation according to the revelation that Jesus gave me, this word translated "Resurrection" 39 times, "raising again," one time, "raised to life again," one time, and "that shall raise," one time. This makes 42 times this word occurs where John said, "Blessed and holy is he that hath part in the first resurrection: on such the second death hath no power, but they shall be priests of God and of Christ, and shall reign with him a thousand years." (Revelation 20:6) This connects the first resurrection with 42, the number for the coming of Jesus. A compound form of the Greek word "anastasis" is found one time in the New Testament; it is "exanastasis." It is found in Philippians 3:11, and is translated "Resurrection."

If this compounded form of anastasis be counted, the 42nd time this word would be found is in Revelation 20:5 where it is said, "This is the first resurrection." In the statement, "This is the first resurrection." there are five Greek words and 20 Greek letters. When the numbers from one to 20 are added up the sum is 210. When this number, 210, is divided by five, the number of words in the passage, it comes out exactly 42, which is the number for the second coming of Jesus.

When Jesus comes to raise His sleeping saints and to translate the living saints then their bodies will be redeemed and the manifestation of the sons of God will take place. "For the earnest expectation of the creature waiteth for the manifestation of the sons of God." (Romans 8:19) At that time it will be brought to light who are really the sons of God.

In the same connection Paul said, "And not only they, but ourselves also, which have the firstfruits of the Spirit, even we ourselves groan within ourselves, waiting for the adoption, to wit, the redemption of our body." See Romans 8:23.

Number 22 stands for light or making manifest, number 20 stands for redemption, and when 22 is added to 20, the sum is 42, for the second coming of Jesus at which time the manifestation of the sons of God will take place and their bodies will be redeemed. Where can such a book as the Bible be found?

The return of Jesus to the earth to reign is also connected with 42. The beast or the man of sin is to be destroyed with the brightness of our Lord's coming. "For the mystery of iniquity doth already work: only he who now letteth will let, until he be taken out of the way. And then shall that Wicked be revealed, whom the Lord shall consume with the spirit of his mouth, and shall destroy with the brighteness of his coming," (II Thessalonians 2:7-8)

There are 36 Greek words in this statement, the exact number of words found about the beast in Revelation 3:2, and the exact number of times the beast is mentioned in the book of Revelation. This also shows that this person will be destroyed with the brightness of our Lord's coming.

In Revelation 13:5, it is stated that the beast will continue 42 months. "and power was given unto him to continue FORTY and TWO months." In Revelation 19:11-21, there is a prophecy of the return of Christ to judge and make war. He is called Faithful and True in the 11th verse, in the 13th verse He is called the Word of God. In the 16th verse, He is called the King of kings and the Lord of lords. In the 19th and 20th verses, He is a prophecy of the beast being cast into the lake of fire and brimstone. So since the beast will continue 42 months and since he will be destroyed at the return of Jesus, then Jesus will return to reign at the end of 42 months of the beast's power, this again connects our Lord's coming with the number 42.

I've just told you something, children of God, Hallelujah! Jesus revealed unto me of His coming and when. Oh, if you can just see what Jesus has revealed to you! That you might know the time of His coming! Not the day nor the hour, but the time of His coming.

Let us see how 42 balances with the number of the devil plus the number of the beast. Here is something to make us marvel indeed. Peter said in I Peter 1:13, "Wherefore gird up the loins of your mind, be sober and hope to the end for the grace that is to be brought unto you at the revelation of Jesus Christ." When five for grace is multiplied by 42 for the coming of Christ, the product is 210. Keep this number in mind.

In Jude, in the 14th and 15th verses, there is a prophecy of Jesus coming in judgment. "And Enoch also, the seventh from Adam, prophesied of these saying, Behold, the Lord cometh with ten thousands of his saints, To execute judgment upon all, and to convince all that are ungodly among them of all their ungodly deeds which they have ungodly committed, and of all their hard speeches which ungodly sinners have spoken against him." Here is a prophecy of Jesus coming in judgment. Number 11 stands for judgment and 42 for the coming of Jesus. When 42 is multiplied by 11, the product is 462. Let this number, also, be kept in mind.

It was Enoch, the seventh from Adam, who prophesied of this judgment. When 462 is divided by seven, the number connected with Enoch, it comes out exactly 66 times. Enoch prophesied of judgment. When you take 11, the number for judgment, and add all the numbers from one to 11, the sum is 66.

A description? This coming in judgment is given in Revelation 19:11-12 and Revelation is the 66th and last book of the Bible.

Now let us add 210 (which was obtained by multiplying 42 for the coming of Jesus, by five, the number for grace as given in I Peter 1:13) to 462 (which is 11, for the judgment, divided by 42, which is for the coming of Jesus). These two numbers, 210 and 462, make 672. Six, the number for the devil or Satan, added to 666, the number of the beast (see Revelation 13:18), equals 672. The evil combination of the devil and the beast will be broken up by our Lord's return.

How about those numbers, children of God? Who could write such a book or books and make them balance like this? Only one inspired by God to do so, by the revelation of Jesus Christ! Each of the 66 books of the Bible was inspired and guided by Him, Who is all-wise and never makes a mistake.

Perdition
"FORTY-FOUR"

Let's take the next number. Forty-four is the number for PERDITION. This is found by reading Revelation 17:9-11. "And here is the mind which hath wisdom. The seven heads are seven mountains, on which the woman sitteth. And there are seven kings: five are fallen, and one is, and the other is not yet come; and when he cometh, he must continue a short space. And the beast that was, and is not, even he is the eighth, and is of the seven, and goeth into perdition."

Seven heads and seven mountains are 14, one woman, seven kings, five have fallen and one to come . . . a sum of 28; even he is the eighth that is to come is 29, the beast that was and is not. Thirty-seven and seven and goeth into PERDITION — that totals 44, which is the number for PERDITION.

In the words, "the beast that was, and is not, even he is the eighth," there are 44 Greek letters. In the words, "and is the seven, and goeth into PERDITION," there are 36 Greek letters. Here is 36, the Enemy, the number of times the beast is mentioned in the book of Revelation. Then there are 44 letters, the number of PERDITION, where he goes in the end. In Revelation 19:20 we read, "And the beast was taken, and with him the false prophet that wrought miracles before him, with which he deceived them that had received the mark of the beast, and them that worshipped his image."

These both were cast alive into a fire burning with brimstone. In this statement there are exactly 44 Greek words, the number for PERDITION where John said he would go. It has been seen that 30 is the number for the Blood of Jesus and when 30 is subtracted from 44, it leaves 14, the number for Salvation. "For God so loved the world, that he gave his only begotten Son, that whosoever believeth in him should not perish, but have everlasting life." That's John 3:16. The one who receives the Love (number 16) of God in his heart will not go to PERDITION (number 44) but will have Eternal Life (number 28). When 16 is subtracted from 44, we get 28, for Eternal Life. When 19, for Faith, is subtracted from 44, for PERDITION, it leaves 25, the Forgiveness of Sins.

The number for the natural or unsaved man is four. Eleven stands for Judgment. When four is multiplied by 11, the product is 44, the number for PERDITION. This is where the unsaved will go after being judged. "And whosoever was not found written in the Book of Life was cast into the Lake of Fire." That is Revelation 20:15. The words "whosoever was not found written in the book of life" have 11 Greek words and 44 Greek letters. That ought to take care of 44 in the precious Name of Jesus.

Inheritance
"FORTY-FIVE"

Let us go on to 45. It is the number connected with Inheritance. In Joshua 14:14, we find where Caleb was given the INHERITANCE which God, through Moses, had promised unto him, 45 years after that promise was made. The name of Caleb is found nine times in the Book of Joshua. When all the numbers from one to nine are added, they total 45.

In Genesis 15:18 we read, "In the same day the Lord made a Covenant with Abram, saying, Unto thy seed have I given this land, from the (1) river of Egypt unto the great (2) river, the (3) river Euphrates:" In this connection, the name of

Abram occurs the 42nd time and the word "River" is found three times. When three is added to 42 that makes 45, the number of INHERITANCE, and that is what is under consideration in this verse.

The names Shadrach, Meshach and Abednego are found 15 times in the book of Daniel. The 15th time is where they were promoted in the Providence of Babylon. This was after they had been brought forth alive out of the fiery furnace. Here is found a picture of the Resurrection.

When we multiply 15, the number of times their names are mentioned, by three, the number of Hebrew children, and the number for the Resurrection, we get 45, the number for INHERITANCE.

In Matthew 5:5 we read, "Blessed are the meek: for they shall inherit the earth." There are 45 Greek letters in this statement, and this is the third one of the Beatitudes. Number 45 is 42 for the Second Coming of Jesus, and three for the Resurrection of the saints which will take place at the Lord's coming. After this the saints will inherit the earth. That ought to be enough for number 45.

Second Death
"FORTY-SIX"

Let me go on. Forty-six is the Second Death. The number 46 seems to be this because it is twice 23, and 23 is the number for the First Death.

So twice 23 should give us the number for the Second Death. That is the only usage I can find in the Bible for 46.

Tabernacle or Dwelling Place
"FORTY-EIGHT"

So let's go on to 48. I'd say 48 is a number connected with a Dwelling Place. In Exodus 25:8 we read where God said to Moses concerning Israel and the Tabernacle, "And let them make me a sanctuary; that I may dwell among them."

By reading Exodus 26:15-25 we find that there are 48 boards in the Wall of the Tabernacle. Twenty on the south side, 20 on the north side and eight on the west end. The east end was closed with a covering of cloth called the Door.

In Joshua 21:41 we read, "All the cities of the Levites within the possession of the children of Israel were *FORTY* and *EIGHT* cities with their suburbs." So the Levites had 48 cities in which to dwell.

As I have stated before, in some places I give only enough to justify the number (not I but the Lord). There are many other places where these numbers all come together.

The Wrath of God
"FORTY-NINE"

Now let's take 49. It is the number connected with the Wrath of God, and it is related in some ways to the great tribulation. The word "Dragon" has been shown to occur 13 times in the book of Revelation and there are 36 references to the beast, and when these two numbers are added, the sum is 49. This is the number I am concerned with now.

In Revelation 15:6-7, John said, "And the seven angels came out of the temple, having the seven plagues, clothed in pure and white linen, and having their breasts girded with golden girdles. And one of the four beasts gave unto the seven angels seven golden vials full of the Wrath of God, who liveth for ever and ever."

Now in this statement there are 49 Greek words. There are seven angels, with seven vials, which are full of the Wrath of God. When seven is multiplied by seven, the product is 49. By reading the 16th chapter of Revelation, it will be seen that the beast and those who worship him and the dragon will be connected with these seven last plagues brought by the seven angels.

The 49th time the word "Earth" is found in Genesis is where it is said, "And it came to pass after seven days, that the waters of the flood were upon the earth." (Genesis 7:10) The flood came because of the Wrath of God upon that generation.

The Spirit, Holy Ghost, and Israel's Jubilee "FIFTY"

The next number is a precious one to me, it is 50 — the Spirit and Jubilee and the Holy Ghost. Fifty is the number connected with the Spirit, Holy Ghost and a Jubilee. Its Spirit was poured out at the first Pentecost after the resurrection of Jesus.

The word "Pentecost" means 50. "And ye shall count unto you from the morrow after the sabbath, from the day that ye brought the sheaf on the wave offering; seven sabbaths shall be complete: Even unto the morrow after the seventh sabbath shall ye number *FIFTY* days; and ye shall offer a new meat offering unto the Lord." That's Leviticus 23:15, 16.

I wonder how many have read that scripture? The sheaf of the firstfruits on the morrow after the Sabbath, of the first day of the week as in Leviticus 23:10-11, representing the resurrection of Jesus. "But now is Christ risen from the dead, and become the firstfruits of them that slept." That's I Corinthians 15:20.

The new meat offering that was offered 50 days after the waving of the firstfruits, representing the outpouring of the Holy Ghost which came 50 days after Jesus' crucifixion. He arose on the first day of the week and the firstfruits were waved before the Lord on the first day of the week or on the morrow after the SABBATH. That's, of course, in Leviticus 23:10, 11.

Now let's go into the Court of the Tabernacle. The court of the Tabernacle was 50 cubits wide. "The length of the Court shall be an hundred cubits, and the breadth *FIFTY* every where, and the height five cubits of fine twined linen," That is Exodus 27:18. Here is seen the number five, for Grace, 50, for the Spirit, Who is called the "Spirit of Grace?" in Hebrews 10:29.

It will be seen that 100 stands for the children of Promise or the Elect. This hanging of the Court that was 50 cubits in length joined up with the hanging of the long side which was 100 cubits long, so does God give the Spirit to everyone everywhere, Whom He calls. "For the promise is unto you, and to your children, and to all that are afar off, even as many as the Lord our God shall call." That's Acts 2:39.

Let's take JUBILEE now. Israel had what is called the year of Jubilee every 50 years. "And thou shalt number seven sabbaths of years unto thee, seven times seven years; and the space of the seven sabbaths of years shall be unto thee forty and nine years. Then shalt thou cause the trumpet of the JUBILEE to sound on the tenth day of the seventh month, in the day of atonement shall ye make the trumpet sound throughout all your land. And ye shall hallow the FIFTIETH year, and proclaim liberty throughout all the land unto all the inhabitants thereof: it shall be a JUBILEE unto you; and ye shall return every man unto his possession, and ye shall return every man unto his family." That's Leviticus 25:8-10.

This year of JUBILEE, in which every man returned unto his own possession, is a picture of the reign of Jesus and His

129

saints, when all Israel shall return to its possessions and the ransomed of the Lord shall return and come to Zion with songs of everlasting joy. I'd say that meant JUBILEE. "And the ransomed of the Lord shall return, and come to Zion with songs and everlasting joy upon their heads: they shall obtain joy and gladness, and sorrow and sighing shall flee away." That's Isaiah 35:10.

Here is the word "ransomed," so that meant "redeemed," and it is connected with Israel's return of JUBILEE. Then when 20, the number for redemption, is multiplied by 50, the number of years connected with the year of JUBILEE, the product is 1000, the number of years of the Millennium reign as in Revelation 20:4-6. The blowing of the trumpet was connected with the year of JUBILEE and the returning of the people to their possessions. "And it shall come to pass in that day, that the Lord shall beat off from the channel of the river unto the stream of Egypt, and ye shall be gathered one by one, O ye children of Israel. And it shall come to pass in that day, that the great trumpet shall be blown, and they shall come which were ready to perish in the land of Assyria, and the outcasts in the land of Egypt, and shall worship the Lord in the holy mount at Jerusalem." That's Isaiah 27:12, 13. "Then shall they know that I am the Lord their God, which caused them to be led into captivity among the heathen: but I have gathered them unto their own land, and have left none of them any more there. Neither will I hide my face any more from them: for I have poured out my spirit upon the house of Israel, saith the Lord God." That's Ezekiel 39:28, 29.

From this it is seen that there is to be an outpouring of the Spirit on Israel bringing great joy. We find that in I Peter 1:1 and in I Thessalonians 1:6. This is why the number 50 is connected both with the Holy Ghost and the years of Jubilee. In the year of Jubilee they were to proclaim liberty throughout all the land. In II Corinthians 3:17 we read, "where the Spirit of the Lord is, there is liberty."

The word of God tells us that creation shall be delivered

from the Bondage into the glorious liberty of the children of
God. See Romans 8:21. Israel shall also have rest from her
bondage in the glorious year of Jubilee, or the 1000-year
reign. See Isaiah 14:1-3. That should do it for number 50.

Oh, my precious Lord. The outpouring came to the Gentiles. It won't be long now until the outpouring upon the
Jews, and the Gentiles cut off. . . .

The Security of the Believer
"FIFTY-FOUR"

Fifty-four is the next number that the Lord would like to
bring forth and it is connected with the Security of the Believer. Yes, the Lord did say that number 54 is the number
connected with the Security of the sons of God. It is 26 for
the Gospel, plus 28 for Eternal Life. It is 12 for Divine Authority, the power by which we are saved and kept, and 42
for the Coming of Christ Jesus, until which time we are kept.
"Being confident of this very thing, that he which hath begun
a good work in you will perform it until the day of Jesus
Christ." That's Philippians 1:6.

It was His Divine Power which began the work in the sons
of God. It is His power that will perform it until the Coming
of Christ. "And the very God of peace sanctify you wholly;
and I pray God your whole spirit and soul and body be
preserved blameless unto the coming of our Lord Jesus
Christ. Faithful is he that calleth you, who also will do it."
That is I Thessalonians 5:23-25.

Here again it is stated that the children of God are preserved by His Divine Power until the second coming of the
Lord, "Who are kept by the power of God through faith unto
salvation ready to be revealed in the last time." That is I
Peter 1:5. It is seen that it is the power of God which keeps
us unto the coming of Christ. When 12, for Divine Power, is

added to 42, for the coming of Christ, they total 54, for the Believer's Security.

Paul said that he who has begun a good work in the believer would perform it, or as some translations read, findeth or complete it at the Day of the Lord.

Peter said that we are kept by the power of God unto salvation ready to be revealed in the last time. In Romans 8:19 we read, "For the earnest expectation of the creature waiteth for the manifestation of the sons of God." In Romans 8:23 we are told that we groan within ourselves waiting for the Redemption of our bodies.

When 12 (Divine Power, which keeps us), 22 (manifest or making light the Son of God) and 20 (the Redemption of our bodies) are all added, they equal 54, the number for the Security of the children of God. By actual count there are 54 Greek words in our Lord's statement about the security of His sheep. "My sheep hear my voice, and I know them, and they follow me: And I give unto them eternal life; and they shall never perish, neither shall any man pluck them out of my hand. My Father, which gave them me, is greater than all; and no man is able to pluck them out of my Father's hand." That is John 10:27-29. The translation of this passage from Greek has exactly 54 English words. If Jesus was not speaking concerning the security of His people, then these words are meaningless.

In the Bible specification of the Tabernacle there are exactly 54 Pillars in the Court. On these 54 pillars there were hangings five cubits high. See Exodus 27:18. Number five stands for Grace. Here is a picture of God's people being shut in on every side by Grace, and that hanging five cubits high hung on 54 pillars of the Court.

In the Court of the Tabernacle there is a picture of the sheepfold about which Jesus was speaking when He said, "there shall be one fold, and one shepherd." (John 10:16) In the passage in John 10:27-29, Jesus made seven positive statements concerning His sheep. (1) He said that they heard His voice, (2) He said that He knew them, (3) He said that they followed Him, (4) He said that He gave them eternal life, (5) He said that they shall never perish, (6) He said that none could pluck them out of His hand, and (7) He said that none were able to pluck them out of the Father's hand. All the words in these seven statements are in the indicative mood both in the Greek and in the English. The indicative mood expresses a positive undoubted fact.

To insert any "if" into any of these statements and make them conditional statements would be to change the mood from indicative to suggestive and thus change the meaning of the Bible words. This is what the *Apostate* teacher does when he says "if" they follow Christ they shall not perish. Jesus did not have the word "if" in any of these statements.

He did not say "if" My sheep follow Me, but He said, "they follow me:" There is a positive statement to the effect that the Lord's sheep do follow Him. He also said in the same chapter, "a stranger will they not follow," That's found in John 10:5. Not only did the Lord say they would follow Him; but He stated that they would not follow a stranger, and then He gave the reason why they would not follow a stranger. For one to argue that they will sometimes follow a stranger is to say they will do something which Jesus said they would not do.

Not only did Jesus say His sheep would not follow a stranger and then give the reason why, but He also gave the reason why the Pharisees did not follow Him. He said to them, "But ye believe not, because ye are not of my sheep, as I said unto you. My sheep hear my voice, and I know them, and they follow me:" The very fact that the Pharisees did not follow Him would serve to prove that they were not of His sheep, because His sheep followed Him and heard His voice. Those who do not follow Him, do not follow Him because they are not of His sheep. It's as simple as that.

Pride
"SIXTY"

Number 60 is seen to be the number that is connected with PRIDE. In the Bible, the Image which Nebuchadnezzar built to be worshipped was 60 cubits high. In Daniel 3:1 you will find this. In the second chapter of Daniel we find that Nebuchadnezzar had a dream in which he saw a great Image.

This Image's head was of fine gold. Its arms and breasts were of silver, its belly and thighs were of brass. Its legs were of iron, and its feet were part iron and part clay.

Daniel told Nebuchadnezzar that he was the head of gold. The next thing about which we read is the erection of this image of gold by Nebuchadnezzar. This indicates that the statement of Daniel to him about him being the head of gold lifted him up with Pride and caused him to make this image.

In speaking to Belshazzar concerning Nebuchadnezzar, Daniel said that his heart was lifted up and his mind was hardened with Pride. You can find this in Daniel 5:8-20.

So it was PRIDE that caused Nebuchadnezzar to build this Image that was 60 cubits high. That ought to take care of number 60. There are other references in the Bible pertaining to 60, but this is all Jesus gave to me for this revelation.

Image or Idol Worship
"SIXTY-SIX"

Let's go on to 66. Sixty-six is the number that is connected with Image or Idol Worship. Nebuchadnezzar made an Image of gold. "whose height was threescore cubits, and the breadth thereof six cubits:" That's Daniel 3:1. Notice the two numbers 60 and six are connected with the Image which Nebuchadnezzar erected to be worshipped.

Jeremiah prophesied that Judah would be taken captive and remain for 70 years. This was because of the tribe's Idol Worship. That is found in Jeremiah 25:4-11. The cause of this captivity and the length of time they would stay in Babylon was foreshadowed by the number who went down into Egypt with Jacob. "All the souls that came with Jacob into Egypt, which came out of his loins, besides Jacob's sons' wives, all the souls were threescore and six; And the sons of Joseph, which were born him in Egypt, were two souls: all the souls of the house of Jacob, which came into Egypt, were threescore and ten." That is in Genesis 46:26, 27.

Now in this passage of scripture the numbers 66 and 70 are found connected with the going down of the House of Israel into Egypt. These two numbers correspond with the numbers for Idol Worship, which is 66, and with the number of years they remained in Babylonian captivity because of their Idol Worship, and their acts of disobedience. Could this have been accidental or was it according to the divine pattern?

Israel's Captivity and Return "SEVENTY"

Number 70 is Israel's Captivity and Return. Seventy is the number connected with Israel's captivity and return. Under the discussion of number 66, number 70 was brought in as the number of years the people of Judah were to stay in Babylonian captivity. That can be found in Jeremiah 25:4-11.

In II Chronicles 36:19-23 we read, "And they burnt the house of God, and brake down the wall of Jerusalem, and burnt all the palaces thereof with fire, and destroyed all the goodly vessels thereof. And them that had escaped from the sword carried he away to Babylon; where they were servants to him and his sons until the reign of the kingdom of Persia:

To fulfil the word of the Lord by the mouth of Jeremiah, until the land had enjoyed her sabbaths: for as long as she lay desolate she kept sabbath, to fulfil threescore and ten years. Now in the first year of Cyrus king of Persia, that the Word of the Lord spoken by the mouth of Jeremiah might be accomplished, the Lord stirred up the spirit of Cyrus king of Persia, that he made a proclamation throughout all his kingdom, and put it also in writing, saying; Thus saith Cyrus king of Persia, All the kingdoms of the earth hath the Lord God of heaven given me; and he hath charged me to build him an house in Jerusalem, which is in Judah. Who is there among you of all his people? The Lord his God be with him, and let him go up.''

So at the end of 70 years in Babylon's captivity, there was a partial and a temporary return of the Jews to their land. The number seven stands for completeness, and if the number 70 was connected with Israel's partial or temporary return, then 70 times seven should be the number connected with ISRAEL's complete and final return. This brings up the study of Daniel's 70 weeks.

Israel's Complete
and Final Restoration
"SEVENTY TIMES SEVEN"

Let us go on to the 70 times seven. This is Israel's complete and final restoration, 70 times seven years or 490 years are connected with Israel's final restoration to her land.

Perhaps one of the hardest prophecies to understand has been Daniel's prophecy concerning the 70 weeks appointed to Israel. This prophecy has been the basis of much controversy. Right here is where the number system is of so much value. In the ninth chapter of Daniel, the prophet Daniel was praying and confessing his sins and the sin of his people, and asking the Lord to look upon the desolation of their land,

and to forgive his people and to take away their reproach.

While he was presenting his supplications before the Lord, the angel Gabriel came and touched him and told him that he had come to give him understanding concerning the things about which he had been praying. Here are the words of the angel to Daniel, "Seventy weeks are determined upon thy people and upon thy holy city, to finish the transgression, and to make an end of sins, and to make reconciliation for iniquity, and to bring everlasting righteousness, and to seal up the vision and prophecy, and to anoint the most Holy. Know therefore and understand, that from the going forth of the commandment to restore and to build Jerusalem unto the Messiah the Prince shall be seven weeks, and threescore and two weeks: the street shall be built again, and the wall, even in troublous times. And after threescore and two weeks shall Messiah be cut off, but not for himself: and the people of the prince that shall come shall destroy the city and the sanctuary; and the end thereof shall be with a flood, and unto the end of the war desolations are determined. And he shall confirm the covenant with many for one week: and in the midst of the week he shall cause the sacrifice and the oblation to cease, and for the overspreading of abominations he shall make it desolate, even until the consummation, and that determined shall be poured upon the desolate." That is Daniel 9:24-27. The translation of this passage by Dr. Alex R. Gordon (Goodspeed translation) reads, "Seventy weeks of years are determined for your people and for your holy city to finish the crime, to end the sin, to experace the guilt, to bring in everlasting righteousness, to confirm the prophetic vision and to consecrate the most sacred place."

In this passage of prophecy, Daniel's prayer for God to forgive Israel's sin and to look upon the desolation of that country, must be taken into consideration. Any interpretation of this prophecy that has these 70 weeks of years ending, leaving Israel desolate, still unforgiven and scattered, cannot be the right interpretation, but this is exactly what the opponents of the premillennium position do. They have these

70 weeks closing with Israel still unforgiven and Daniel's prayer unanswered. The war is to continue till the end of time. Dr. Gordon's translation of the passage reads, "The end shall be with a flood, with wars raging to the end." Wars are still raging so we have not yet come to the end of this period of time. Any interpretation of this passage must take into consideration the 70 Sabbath years that Israel failed to observe and for which the people are to be punished. They were commanded to have a Sabbath year for the land every seven years. "But in the seventh year shall be a sabbath of rest unto the land, a sabbath for the Lord: thou shalt neither sow thy field, nor prune thy vineyard." That is Leviticus 25:4. Israel failed to observe 70 Sabbath years. Seventy Sabbath years would reach over a period of 490 years or 70 times seven years. Read II Chronicles 36:19-21. So Daniel's 70 years must be 70 weeks of years. That would total 490 years, which would be the length of time which Israel did not observe a Sabbath year.

Next, since the land of Israel was involved in the observances of those Sabbath years, then we should expect God's blessing to be upon the land again at the end of the 70 weeks of years. Many passages in the Psalms and the Prophets indicate that this is what will take place. "I will hear what God the LORD will speak: for He will speak peace unto his people, and to his saints: but let them not turn again to folly. Surely his salvation is nigh them that fear Him; that glory may dwell in our land. Mercy and truth are met together; righteousness and peace have kissed each other. Truth shall spring out of the earth; and righteousness shall look down from heaven. Yea the LORD shall give that which is good; and our land shall yield her increase." That is Psalm 85:8-12.

In connection with the Lord's promise to cleanse Israel from all her sins there is also a promise to bless her land. "For I will take you from among the heathen, and gather you out of all countries, and will bring you into your own land. Then will I sprinkle clean water upon you, and ye shall be clean: from all your filthiness and from all your idols, will I cleanse you. A new heart also will I give you, and a new spirit will I put within you: and I will take away the stony heart out of your flesh, and I will give you an heart of flesh. And I will put my spirit within you, and cause you to walk in my statutes, and ye shall keep my judgments, and do them. And ye shall dwell in the land that I gave to your fathers; and ye shall be my people, and I will be your God. I will also save you from all your uncleannesses; and I will call for the corn, and will increase it, and lay no famine upon you. And I will multiply the fruit of the tree, and the increase of the field, that ye shall receive no more reproach of famine among the heathen." That is Ezekiel 36:24-30.

From these scriptures it is seen that along with the forgiveness of Israel and her cleansing from sin there is a promise of God's blessing upon the land of Israel. Her punishment and exile are connected with her failure to keep 490 years of 70 Sabbath years (God's command to let the land rest every seventh year). The length of time they failed to observe the Sabbath corresponds exactly with Daniel's 70 weeks of years.

Jesus used the expression "seventy times seven" in speaking of forgiving trespasses. "Then came Peter to him, and said, Lord, how oft shall my brother sin against me, and I forgive him? Till seven times? Jesus saith unto him, I say not unto thee, Until seven times: but, Until seventy times seven." That is Matthew 18:21-22. So the number 70 times seven is connected with forgiveness, not with putting one away without forgiveness.

Those who would have Israel and the 70 weeks end with the destruction of Jerusalem by Cyrus and the dispersion of Israel are out of harmony with what Jesus said about forgiving until 70 times seven. Surely there is a deeper significance to the 70 times seven spoken by our Lord in this place than might appear on the surface. It equals the number of years during which Israel disobeyed the Lord concerning the command about the Sabbath year. It equals in number Daniel's 70 weeks.

Having taken into consideration the things just mentioned,

let us examine the passage itself. It will be seen that Daniel divided the 70 weeks into three groups. There are seven weeks, 62 weeks and one week. The last week is divided into parts, "Know therefore and understand, that from the going forth of the commandment to restore and to build Jerusalem unto the Messiah, the Prince shall be seven weeks, and threescore and two weeks: the street shall be built again, and the wall, even in troublous times. And after threescore and two weeks shall Messiah be cut off, but not for himself: and the people of the prince that shall come shall destroy the city and the sanctuary; and the end thereof shall be with a flood, and unto the end of the war desolations are determined. And he shall confirm the covenant with many for one week: and in the midst of the week [which would be the middle] he shall cause the sacrifice and the oblation to cease, and for the overspreading of the abominations he shall make it desolate, even until the consummation, and that determined shall be poured upon the desolate." (Daniel 9:25-27)

Now the 70 weeks started with the command of Cyrus for the city of Jerusalem to be rebuilt as found in II Chronicles 36:22-23. The seven weeks went until the wall was rebuilt in the days of Nehemiah; then after 62 more weeks, the Messiah, or Christ, was cut off upon the rejection of Jesus in Israel. At His crucifixion Israel's clock stopped, not to start again until the fullness of the times of the Gentiles has come in.

By reading Matthew 23:27-29 and Luke 19:41-44, we will find that just a few days before our Lord's crucifixion Jesus wept over Jerusalem and turned His back on the city and abandoned it to its fate until they say, "Blessed is he that cometh in the name of the Lord." (Luke 13:35) Now, by reading Romans 11:25, we find that temporary blindness has come upon Israel to last until the fullness of the Gentiles has come in. Therefore, we must go beyond the close of the Gentile's age for the 70th week or the last seven years. The one who shall come is evidently the Antichrist, or beast of Revelation, who will make a covenant with many of the Jews for one week, which is the last or seventh week.

In the middle of this week he shall break the covenant and set abomination and desolation. In Matthew 24:15-22, Jesus connected the abomination or desolation spoken of by Daniel with the great tribulation period. So the last half of this 70 weeks of years will be the three and one-half years of Israel's great tribulation.

According to Revelation 11:1-2, Jerusalem is to be trodden down for 42 months after the temple has been rebuilt. Now — this is according to Revelation 13:5 — the beast is to continue 42 months or three and one-half years. According to Revelation 12:14, Israel is to be persecuted for a time, times and a half time by the dragon. That's in Revelation 13:1-2.

We learn here that the dragon will give to the beast his power. So this is all the same period of time, and the beast will be the instrument through which the dragon or devil will persecute the woman of the twelfth chapter of Revelation for three and one-half years. The woman in this chapter represents Israel. She brought forth the man child who is to rule all nations with a rod of iron. (Revelation 12:1-5)

By reading Revelation 19:11-15, we find that the man child is Jesus. All this leads to the consideration of the numbers with the dragon in the twelfth chapter of Revelation. "And there appeared another wonder in heaven; and behold a great red dragon, having seven heads and ten horns, and seven crowns upon his heads." That is Revelation 12:3. Here we have the numbers seven and ten and seven connected with the dragon, who will persecute the woman or Israel for this three and one-half years. When the seven, ten and seven are multiplied, they equal 490 or 70 times seven.

Now this points to the last part of Daniel's prophecy of 70 weeks as the time the dragon will persecute Israel. Now if you will notice the order in which these numbers come, they are seven and ten and seven, not seven and seven and ten. Seven times ten is 70 and seven times 70 is 490. So the numbers are the same as we find in Daniel's prophecy of the

70 weeks that are determined upon Israel.

When Jesus has returned to earth to overthrow the dragon and the beast, then wars will end. Israel will be forgiven and completely restored to her land where for a period of 490 years they sinned against the Lord in failing to observe a Sabbath year.

Vengeance
"SEVENTY-SEVEN"

And now let us go on into number 77, Vengeance. Seventy-seven was referred twice to me by Jesus the Lord in the Word of God as line upon line it is connected with VENGEANCE. The first one is in Genesis 4:23-24: "And Lamech said unto his wives, Adah and Zillah, Hear my voice; ye wives of Lamech, hearken unto my speech; for I have slain a man to my wounding, and a young man to my hurt. If Cain shall be avenged sevenfold, truly Lamech *SEVENTY* and *SEVEN*-fold."

The other reference is Judges 8:1-16, where Gideon took vengeance on threescore and 17 or 77 Elders of the city of Succoth because they refused to give food to his men when he was pursuing the Midianites. This indicates that 77 is the number connected with VENGEANCE.

Casting Out
"NINETY-ONE"

Let us go on to the number which is 91. Ninety-one is connected with Casting Out. It has been shown that the word "Dragon" occurs 13 times in the book of Revelation. The

13th time it occurs is in Revelation 20:2. In that connection we read, "And he laid hold on the dragon, that old serpent, which is the Devil, and Satan, and bound him a thousand years. And cast him into the bottomless pit, and shut him up, and set a seal upon him, that he should deceive the nations no more, till the thousand years should be fulfilled:" That is Revelation 20:2, 3.

Here we find the dragon cast into the bottomless pit in the place where the word "Dragon" occurs the 13th time in the book of Revelation. It has already been seen that all the numbers from one to 13 add up to 91. In Galatians 4:30 we read, "Nevertheless what saith the scripture? Cast out the bondwoman and her son: for the son of the bondwoman shall not be heir with the son of the freewoman." This statement contains 91 Greek letters. Ishmael, the son of the bondwoman, was circumcised when he was 13 years old. That is found in Genesis 17:25. It is not accidental that the number connected with Ishmael's circumcision corresponds with the number of times the word "Dragon" occurs in the book of Revelation, nor that 91 Greek letters are found in the statement about Ishmael's being cast out. This is exactly the same number we get when we add all the numbers from one to 13.

I've brought out that there are 36 references to the beast in Revelation and that the word "Dragon" occurs 13 times in the book of Revelation. In Revelation 13:5-23, we find that the beast is to continue 42 months. At the end of those 42 months, the beast is to be cast into the lake of fire and the dragon into the bottomless pit. That is in Revelation 19:20, and it goes right through Revelation 20:3. When these numbers 13, 36 and 42 are added, they total 91. These numbers would not work out this way unless they were arranged by Divine pattern and design.

143

Seal
"NINETY-NINE"

Ninety-nine is to be connected with a Seal or Sealing, for in Genesis 17:24, we learn that Abraham was circumcised when he was 99 years old. Then in Romans 4:11 we read where Paul said he received the sign of circumcision, a seal of righteousness of the Faith while he was yet uncircumcised. That seems to be all that the Lord gave for this number at the present time. Much more can be revealed by studies of the Word of the Living God.

The Elect
"ONE HUNDRED"

Let us go on to 100. One hundred is connected with election, and it really signifies those who are the Elect. God chose or Elected that Jesus should come of the lineage of Arphaxad, the son of Shem.

By reading Genesis 11:10-27, it will be seen that Abraham was in the lineage of Arphaxad. In Genesis 11:10 we read, "Shem was an hundred years old, and begat Arphaxad two years after the flood:" Here the numbers 100 and two are connected with Arphaxad.

It has been seen that two is connected with Division and Separation. Here is the line from whom Jesus should come. Isaac was an Elected or Chosen person. God said to Abraham, "in Isaac shall thy seed be called." (Genesis 21:12) In Romans 9:7-12, Paul connects Isaac and Jacob with the doctrine of Election: "Neither, because they are the seed of Abraham, are they all children: but, in Isaac shall thy seed be called. That is, They which are the children of the flesh, these are not the children of God: but the children of the promise are counted for the seed. For this is the word of promise, At this time will I come, and Sarah shall have a son. And not only this; but when Rebecca also had conceived by one, even by our father Isaac; (For the children being not yet born, neither having done any good or evil, that the purpose of God according to election might stand, not of works, but of him that calleth;) It was said unto her, The elder shall serve the younger."

Here we see Isaac and Jacob connected with God's Election, and Isaac is especially said to represent the children of Promise. "Now we, brethren, as Isaac was, are the children of Promise." Isaac was born when Abraham was 100 years old, "And Abraham was an HUNDRED years old, when his son Isaac was born unto him." (Genesis 21:5)

In this place the name of Isaac occurs the fifth time. It has been seen that five stands for Grace. So we have both numbers, 100 and five, connected with the birth of Isaac. Here we have the Election of Grace. (See Romans 11:5.)

The number 100 is also connected with Isaac in Genesis 26:12. "Then Isaac sowed in that land, and received in the same year an hundredfold: and the Lord blessed him." In the parable of the lost sheep, Jesus used the number 100. "How think ye? if a man have an hundred sheep, and one of them be gone astray, doeth he not leave the ninety and nine, and goeth into the mountains, and seeketh that which is gone astray? And if so be that he find it, verily I say unto you, he rejoiceth more of that sheep, than of the ninety and nine which went not astray." That's Matthew 18:12. Jesus called the Elect His sheep. "And other sheep I have, which are not of this fold: them also I must bring, and they shall hear my voice; and there shall be one fold, and one shepherd." That is found in John 10:16. "My sheep hear my voice, and I know them, and they follow me: And I give unto them eternal life; and they shall never perish, neither shall any man pluck them out of my hand." That is John 10:27, 28. "Now we, brethren as Isaac was, are the children of Promise."

145

Calling on the Name of the Lord
"ONE HUNDRED FIVE"

All right, let's go on to the next number. Praise God, what perfection! The next number to talk about is 105. The number 105 is connected with Calling on the Name of the Lord. "And to Seth, to him also there was born a son; and he called his name Enos: then began men to call upon the name of the Lord." That's Genesis 4:26.

It has been shown that 14 is the number for Salvation and that all the numbers from one to 14 add up to 105. Romans 10:13 states, "For whosoever shall call upon the name of the Lord shall be saved."

That is all the Lord gave to me on this number, but it seems to be sufficient for number 105.

Warfare
"SIX HUNDRED"

Number 600 in the Bible is connected with Warfare. "And he took SIX HUNDRED chosen chariots, and all the chariots of Egypt, and captains over every one of them." That is in Exodus 14:7. Six hundred soldiers of the Tribe of Dan were sent to capture the city of Laish. That's in Judges 18:7-11. Six hundred of the soldiers of Benjamin escaped slaughter by fleeing into the Rock of Rimmon. That's also in Judges 20:46, 47. The head of the spear of Goliath, the Philistines' Champion, weighed 600 shekels of iron. See I Samuel 30:1-18.

I believe from all this that we might safely come to the conclusion that the number 600 represents Warfare, for this was all that was revealed to me by the Lord of this number hidden from the foundation of the world.

Number of the Beast
"SIX HUNDRED SIXTY-SIX"

Let's talk about the number of the BEAST, 666. In Revelation 13:18, "Here is wisdom. Let him that hath understanding count the number of the beast: for it is the number of a man; and his number is SIX HUNDRED THREESCORE AND SIX."

In Revelation 13:8: "And all that dwell upon the earth shall worship him, whose names are not written in the book of Life of the Lamb slain from the foundation of the world." Here we are told that the number of the beast is "SIX HUNDRED THREESCORE AND SIX," or 666. We are also admonished to count the number of the beast. This could be impossible without the knowledge of the Bible system of numbers.

To understand this, one must give himself to the study of the Bible and the Bible system of numbers. For over 30 years, I have studied the Bible and I have found that through my study of the Bible a very important factor of numbers has been brought forth. I've looked up every way, shape and form, that I might know the number of the Beast. I believed that somewhere in the Bible itself the key was to be found and I wanted to find that key, that I might unlock the door, that I might know the coming of Jesus Christ. And as I studied, prayed and fasted and sought the Lord Jesus, one day in the little church in the country where I was abiding at night, Jesus brought this revelation unto me. I know that this key, this Jesus Christ that I worshipped, glorified and was a slave to, would unlock the mystery for me. I never found it until He first, Himself, Jesus, Christ, made me to understand the numbers of the Bible. He opened up a revelation of each number. Having learned the significance of many of the Bible numbers, one night while I was there in the little church, I ran across the count that satisfied me and would satisfy any Bible student.

147

This count was found in Revelation 17:9-14. While Revelation 13:18 which tells us of the number of the beast starts with the expression, "Here is wisdom." Revelation 17:9 begins, "And here is the mind which hath wisdom." In this statement, "Here is wisdom." there are 14 Greek letters. This is the number for SALVATION. Only those with salvation possess the wisdom to understand the *MYSTERY* of God's Word. Yes, with salvation they will understand. They will then be filled with the Holy Ghost as it tells you in Acts 2:38. He said, "Repent [salvation], and be baptized every one of you in the Name of Jesus Christ, for the remission of sins and ye shall receive the gift of the Holy Ghost." The word is God. "In the beginning was the Word, and the Word was with God, and the Word was God." (John 1:1)

The words "And here is the mind that hath wisdom" have 19 Greek letters; this is the number for FAITH. Faith is necessary to the understanding of the Word of God. Now, let us read the whole passage. "And here is the mind which hath wisdom. The seven heads are seven mountains, on which the woman sitteth. And there are seven kings: five are fallen, and one is, and the other is not yet come; and when he cometh, he must continue a short space. And the beast that was, and is not, even he is the eighth, and is of the seven, and goeth into perdition. And ten horns which thou sawest are ten kings, which have received no kingdom as yet; but receive power as kings one hour with the beast. These have one mind, and shall give their power and strength unto the beast. These shall make war with the Lamb, and the Lamb shall overcome them: for he is Lord of lords, and King of kings: and they that are with him are called, and chosen, and faithful."

Now let us find out about the numbers: seven heads, seven mountains, one woman, seven kings and five that are fallen, one is and one is not yet come, and eight the beast that was and is not and is of the seven, and goeth into perdition. Ten horns, one hour, and hath one mind and give their power to the beast, 600 for the war and the ten kings that made war

148

with the Lamb. That totals 666, the number of the BEAST.

Notice the numbers five, eight and ten. These numbers correspond in the order in which they are found in the list. There are 14 numbers in the list which I just gave you and they all add up to 666. The fifth one is five, the eighth one is eight, and the tenth one is ten. These three numbers — five, eight and ten — add up to 23, which has been found to be the number for DEATH.

In Revelation 13:5, where the beast is mentioned the 14th time, we find that the penalty for refusing to worship the beast will be death. "And there was given unto him a mouth speaking great things and blasphemies; and power was given unto him to continue forty and two months." In this place the BEAST is mentioned the 14th time, and the 14th time he is mentioned we find that the penalty for not worshipping his image will be death, death of the soul, loss of salvation.

The 14th time the BEAST is mentioned corresponds with the numbers in the list which add up to 666. The numbers that correspond with themselves — five, eight and ten — add up to 23, the number for death, the penalty for not worshipping the image of the beast.

There are 14 numbers in the list. Fourteen is the number for salvation, and the BEAST will make war with those who have salvation. "it was given unto him to make war with the saints, and to overcome them:" That is Revelation 13:7.

Number five stands for Grace and only those with grace will refuse to worship the image and will allow themselves to be put to death. Number eight stands for the new birth and the ones who will suffer death for refusing to worship the beast and his image will be born-again people. Number ten stands for the Law, and the Law forbids the worship of images. In what I have just said the number seven is found four times. Number four stands for the natural man, one who belongs to the old creation. Number seven stands for completeness or to bring a thing to an end.

The reign of the beast will bring to an end the rule of the natural man. Never after this will an unsaved man rule or reign on this earth after that. Jesus and the glorified saints will rule the earth.

Number four and number seven add up to 11, the number for judgment. Upon His return to earth, the Lord will execute judgment upon the beast and his setup. "And I saw heaven opened, and behold a white horse; and he that sat upon him was called Faithful and True, and in righteousness he doth judge and make war. His eyes were as a flame of fire, and on his head were many crowns; and he had a name written, that no man knew, but he himself. And he was clothed with a vesture dipped in blood: and his name is called The Word of God. And the armies which were in heaven followed him upon white horses, clothed in fine linen, white and clean. And out of his mouth goeth a sharp sword, that with it he should smite the nations: and he shall rule them with a rod of iron: and he treadeth the winepress of the fierceness and wrath of Almighty God. And he hath on his vesture and on his thigh a name written, KING OF KINGS, AND LORD OF LORDS. And I saw an angel standing in the sun; and he cried with a loud voice, saying to all the fowls that fly in the midst of heaven, Come and gather yourselves together unto the supper of the great God; That ye may eat the flesh of kings, and the flesh of captains, and the flesh of mighty men, and the flesh of horses, and of them that sit on them, and the flesh of all men, both free and bond, both small and great. And I saw the *BEAST*, and the kings of the earth, and their armies, gathered together to make war against him that sat on the horse, and against his army. And the beast was taken, and with him the false prophet that wrought miracles before him, with which he deceived them that had received the mark of the beast, and them that worshipped his image. These both were cast alive into a lake of fire burning with brimstone. And the remnant were slain with the sword of him that sat upon the horse, which sword proceeded out of his mouth: and all the fowls were filled with their flesh." That is Revelation 19:11-21.

It has been seen that there are 36 references to the beast in the book of Revelation and all the numbers from one to 36 add up to 666, the number of the beast. This is two counts that add up to 666, the number of the beast. It has been seen that 66 stands for idol worship; number 600 stands for warfare.

In Revelation 13:15, we find that there will be an image made of the beast. When 66, for idol or image worship, is added to 600, for warfare, they total 666, the number of the beast. This is three counts. In II Thessalonians 2:4, we find that the man of sin or beast will exalt himself above God. Here is Pride. In Revelation 13:2, we read there the dragon or devil will give him his power. Then in Revelation 13:7, we read where he is to make war on the saints. When six for the devil, 60 for pride, and 600 for warfare are added, that makes 666, the number of the beast. That's four counts.

In Revelation 17:11 we read that the beast will go into perdition. We have found that the number for perdition is 44. In Revelation 19:19-20, we find that he will be overcome and cast into perdition, at the dawning of the day of God Almighty. Read Revelation 16:13-14; this will bring to light the true character of the beast. When 22 for light, 44 for perdition and 600 for warfare are added, they make 666, the number of the Beast. This is five counts.

In this same connection, the devil is to be bound and the Lord comes back at this time, and when we add six, the devil's number, 18 for binding or bondage, 42 for the coming of Jesus, and 600 for warfare they total 666 again! This makes six counts. Six is the number for the devil who will give to the beast his power. In the last count we have the devil's number which is six. The battle or war is seen in Revelation 19:11-21. And 600 is the number for warfare. The Lord returns in this same connection, and 42 is the number of the Lord's coming. The devil will be bound, and 18 has been found to be the number for binding or bondage. Leave out any one of these factors and the numbers will not add up to 666, the number of the beast who gets his power from the devil.

The devil is to be overcome at this time. All these things tie up with the coming of Jesus, the Battle of the great day of the Almighty or Armageddon, the overthrow of the beast, the binding of Satan — all in the same connection. So Jesus must return before the devil is bound. This shows that Jesus must return before the 1000 years. Thus the devil is bound before the 1000-year reign, so that the coming of Jesus is pre-millennium. This shows the value of the Bible system of numbers. They establish the truth in such a way that there is no other way of answering it. Post-millennium, ante-millennium, or anything else cannot possibly adjust the numbers system to its theory. It has got to be pre-millennium just as the numbers bring it to us.

If they think they can change it, let them try. I have brought it forth with the numbers system. Oh, I didn't do it on my own! I did it by Jesus Christ of Nazareth! Only that which is true and scriptural can be made to conform to this Bible system of numbers. Yours truly, Brother Don, has long thought that there was some way revealed in the Bible to definitely establish what is true, and in a way that the opponents of the truth would be baffled. I have found just that in this Bible system of numbers. Thank You, Jesus!

Anyone can see that the Bible System of Numbers is baffling to infidels, and atheists, and modernists. They would be willing to admit the same. But the same system exposes their theories and private interpretations concerning the position of the Bible. Now what will they do? Throw away the invincible weapon against infidelity and modernism? Or will they accept the same and give up their false position on prophecy? Children of God, Jesus gave me a revelation. Hallelujah! Oh, it is the truth. In Spirit and in Truth.

Confirmation
of the Ark and Flood

These are notes which I would like to add to this book for I feel they will be of great importance to you in further studies that you may wish to make. First, however, I wanted to put the numbers in order as they are given in this book by the Lord God. Glory to God. Hallelujah!

I am going to bring forth now some other things that I believe, as I have said, should be brought forth pertaining to the numbers. The Bible account of Noah's Ark and the Flood has been denied, ridiculed and laughed at by the enemies of the Bible. The Bible writers have been accused of borrowing their accounts of the flood from Babylonian myths.

Since the flood actually took place, and since Noah built the Ark, then it is only natural that different nations of people would have some traditional story about the same. But the Bible's account is the true and accurate account, and it was given by Divine inspiration. This is abundantly confirmed by the use of the Bible numbers, and in a way to baffle the wisdom of this world. The accuracy and precision with which the Bible numbers fit into the account of the Ark and the Flood is something which the wisdom of this world cannot gainsay. Any man who will say that these things are accidental will only expose his own ignorance and lack of reasoning. It has already been shown in this work that I have received according to the Lord through the numbers that the 24th time the Ark is mentioned is where Noah and all in the Ark came out after the flood.

You will find that in Genesis 8:18, 19. It has been shown that the numbers from one to 24 add up to 300 and that the Ark was 300 cubits long. That is in Genesis 6:15. Second, it has been shown that the eighth time the ark was mentioned is where God called the eight members of Noah's family into the Ark. That is in Genesis 7:1. Third, it has been shown that the seventh time the Ark was mentioned it was the 17th day of the month. That is Genesis 8:4. Fourth, it has been shown that the 27th time Noah's name is mentioned it was the 27th day of the month. See Genesis 8:13, 14.

Fifth, number 12 has been shown to be the number connected with Divine Authority, and the 12th time the Ark is mentioned is where they went in the Ark by God's Divine command. That is in Genesis 7:15, 16. Sixth, it has been shown that the number 11 is connected with judgment. It has also been shown that the judgment of the flood came after the birth of the 11th generation: Shem, Ham, and Japheth.

Seventh, it has been shown that the number 23 is connected with death. The 23rd time Noah's name occurs is where it tells about everything dying except Noah and those with him in the Ark. The tenth time Noah's name occurs is where God tells Noah that He is going to destroy all flesh because of man's sins. (Genesis 6:12, 13)

When 13, the number for sin, is added to ten for the tenth time Noah's name is found that again makes 23, for death. Eighth, the number eight has been shown to stand for the new birth or new beginning. God spared eight persons in the Ark to repopulate the earth a new or the second time.

Ninth, it has been shown that five stands for grace and the fifth time Noah's name occurs is where it is said, "But Noah found grace in the eyes of the Lord." (Genesis 6:8)

Tenth, number seven has been shown to stand for completeness and perfection. The seventh time Noah's name is found is where it is said, "Noah was a just man and perfect in

154

this generation." That is Genesis 6:9. Eleventh, it has been shown that Noah prepared an Ark for the saving of his house by the which he condemned the world and the 11th time Noah's name is found is where he made the Ark as God commanded him and in so doing condemned the world. See Genesis 6:22.

Twelfth, it has been shown that 12 stands for Divine Authority, and the 12th time Noah's name is found is where God called to Noah and his family to come into the ark. They went in as God commanded them. See Genesis 7:16. This has already been mentioned. Thirteenth, it has been shown that 13 stands for sin. The flood came upon man because of his great sin. The 13th time the Ark is mentioned is where it says, "And the flood was forty days upon the earth; and the waters increased, and bare up the Ark, and it was lift up above the earth." (Genesis 7:17)

Fourteenth, it has been shown that 14 stands for salvation. There were 14 kinds of clean animals saved in the Ark. It was the same of every clean fowl, and of every clean beast. "And the Lord said unto Noah, Come thou and all thy house into the Ark; for thee have I seen righteous before me in this generation. Of every clean beast thou shalt take to thee by sevens, the male and his female: and of beasts that are not clean by two, the male and his female." See Genesis 7:1, 2. Seven males and seven females would be 14 clean animals or fowls. This is the number for salvation. And the animals, being clean animals, create the picture of the condition of the ones before God who are being saved. Hallelujah!

Fifteenth, the length of the Ark has been shown to be the distance around the court of the Tabernacle. The width of the Ark has been shown to be the width of the court of the Tabernacle. The height of the Ark has been shown to be the length of the court of the Tabernacle.

The Ark had three stories; the Tabernacle had three parts — the court, the Holy Place and the Most Holy Place. See Genesis 6:15 and Exodus 26:15-20, also Exodus 27:9-18.

Sixteenth, the name of Noah is mentioned the 13th time

where he took of the clean animals and offered sacrifices upon the altar which he built. See Genesis 8:20. Number 30 has been seen to represent the blood of Jesus which was shed for the sins of man.

Seventeenth, just two words after the Ark is mentioned the 24th time, Noah's name occurs the 13th time and Noah is found officiating as a priest and offering sacrifice. See Genesis 8:20. The number 24 is connected with the priesthood (in II Chronicles 24:1-19), and the number 30 is connected with the Blood of Jesus (in Matthew 27:3, 4).

Eighteenth, the number 29 has been seen to connect with departure and the 29th time Noah's name occurs is where he went forth out of the Ark. That is in Genesis 8:19.

Nineteenth, the Ark rested on the mountain of Ararat on the 17th day of the month. It has been shown that Jesus arose from the dead on the 17th day of the month. See Genesis 8:4.

Twentieth, the earth is mentioned the 49th time in Genesis 7:10: "And it came to pass after seven days, that the waters of the flood were upon the earth." The flood was indicative of God's wrath upon the earth. In Revelation 16:1, the angels with the seven vials were told to go their way and pour out the vial of God's wrath upon the earth.

Twenty-first, the number four has been shown to stand for the natural man of the flesh. In Genesis 6:12 we read, "for all flesh has corrupted his way upon the earth." In speaking of the Days of Noah, Jesus said, "And as it was in the days of Noe, so shall it be also in the days of the Son of man. They did eat, they drank, they married wives, they were given in marriage, until the day that Noe entered into the ark, and the flood came, and destroyed them all. Likewise also as it was in the days of Lot: they did eat, they drank, they bought, they sold, they planted, they builded; But the same day that Lot went out of Sodom it rained fire and brimstone from heaven, and destroyed them all." That is Luke 17:26-29.

Twenty-second, we have four things mentioned which they were doing in that time, and four represents the flesh which had corrupted his way upon the earth.

Twenty-third, in Genesis 7:10, it is said, "And it came to pass after seven days, that the waters of the flood were upon the earth." Just following this statement, it tells about all dying except Noah and those in the Ark with him. (Verses 21-23) In this place the Ark is mentioned the 15th time, coinciding with the number of cubits that the water had prevailed upward. I challenge any man to count up letters and words and names and show where Brother Don has in any way misrepresented these things. In the face of so much numeral evidence connected with Noah, the flood and the Ark, how can any man be foolish enough to deny the Divine inspiration of the account of the flood?

An atheist wrote me one time and he said that with one little window in the Ark for ventilation, everything in the Ark would have smothered to death in an hour's time. There was no evidence that the window was ever opened until Noah opened it to let the raven and dove out. That is in Genesis 8:6-12. So the window was not used for ventilation. There must have been some other means by which the Ark was ventilated. Enough is given in the Divine record to prove that beyond a shadow of a doubt that the account of the flood and of the Ark is true. But God did not take up any unnecessary space in His Word to gratify all the curious and deprived mankind. That in itself is a mark of Divine inspiration. Had this record been the work of man, he would have wasted many pages seeking to gratify all the curiosity of the lost man. Children of God, I know that the God above wrote only those things necessary to the salvation of eternal life of man by the wisdom and knowledge of His precious Word, which is governed by the numeral system of the Holy Bible.

Confirmation of the Resurrection

Now, I want to confirm the Resurrection of Jesus Christ. The resurrection of Jesus Christ is the foundation stone of the Christian faith and hope. Paul stated that Jesus Christ was declared to be the Son of God with power according to the Spirit of Holiness by the Resurrection from the dead. See Romans 1:1-14.

When the resurrection of Jesus Christ is established, then the believer's faith and hope are confirmed. If Jesus Christ did not rise, then Jesus was no more than some other great religious leader and teacher and our faith is vain. "And if Christ be not risen, then is our preaching vain, and your faith is also vain." (I Corinthians 15:14) If it can be established that Jesus did rise from the dead, then Jesus is lifted up far above all other religious teachers and leaders. He is the Resurrection and the Life. He is God, the Father Almighty! Oh, He is the everlasting unto the everlasting!

Other religious teachers may have put forth some great moral principle, but they did not have the power over death and the grave. Jesus Christ, however, by His Resurrection from the dead, forever establishes His claim to be the Resurrection and the Life. Not only did the writers of the New Testament confirm over and over the Resurrection of Jesus, but their testimony is abundantly confirmed by the Bible system of numbers.

It has been seen that the number three is connected with the Resurrection over and over again and Jesus Himself predicted that He would rise again in three days. "For as Jonas was three days and three nights in the whale's belly; so shall the Son of man be three days and three nights in the heart of the earth." That's Matthew 12:40. Speaking of the temple of His body, "Jesus answered and said unto them. Destroy this Temple, and in three days I will raise it up." That is John 2:19.

When Peter's name occurred the third time in the book of

Acts, he stood up and preached on the outpouring of the Holy Ghost and the Resurrection of Jesus Christ in Acts 2:14-36. In that sermon on the resurrection of Jesus, Peter quoted from the prophecy of David on the Resurrection of the Lord. In that connection, he mentioned David's name three times. (See Acts 2:25; 2:29 and 2:34.)

The third time Jesus showed Himself to His disciples after He had risen from the dead, the disciples had a catch of 153 fish. "Simon Peter went up, and drew the net to land full of great fishes, an hundred and fifty-three:" (See John 21:11.) "This is now the third time that Jesus showed himself to his disciples, after that he was risen from the dead." (John 21:14)

Jesus Christ was raised from the dead on the 17th day of the month. In the Bible a day was reckoned from one evening to the next evening, "the evening and the morning were the first day." (See Genesis 1:5.) The Passover was observed in the evening of the 14th day of the first month or at the beginning of the 14th day. "In the fourteenth day of the first month at even is the Lord's passover." (See Leviticus 23:5.)

The night our Lord was betrayed He ate the Passover supper with His disciples. "And when the hour was come, he sat down, and the twelve apostles with him. And he said unto them, With desire I have desired to eat this passover with you before I suffer." (See Luke 22:14, 15.) "And he took bread, and gave thanks, and brake it, and gave unto them, saying, This is my body which is given for you: this do in remembrance of me. Likewise also the cup after supper, saying, This cup is the new testament in my blood, which is shed for you." (Luke 22:19, 20)

In I Corinthians 11:23-25, it is stated that this is the same night that the Lord was betrayed and was taken before the Sanhedrin court and condemned. When it was day, He was taken before Pilate and condemned and crucified. So Jesus died on the 14th day of the month and was risen three days later according to the Bible record. That would put His Resurrection on the 17th day of the month. This number has

159

been proven to stand for Victory. In His Resurrection, Jesus became victorious over death and the grave.

When all the numbers from one to 17 are added they total 153, the exact number of fish caught on the day that Jesus showed Himself to His disciples the third time after He had risen from the dead. When 17 is multiplied by three, the number for the Resurrection, the product is 51. When 51 is multiplied by three for the third time Jesus showed Himself after His resurrection, we again get 153, the number of fish caught that day.

When Jesus spoke to John on the Isle of Patmos, He said to him, "I am he that liveth, and was dead; and behold, I am alive for evermore, Amen; and have the keys of hell and of death." See Revelation 1:18. Here Christ made three statements about His death, and His Resurrection from the dead. These three things are followed by the word, "Amen;" and this is the third Amen in the book of Revelation.

The arrangement of the numbers that Jesus just gave you was not coincidental; but was according to the Divine pattern and purpose, even as the arrangement of the numbers is connected with the account of Noah's Ark and the flood. These things were arranged in this matter to confound the wisdom of men and to confirm the truth of God's Word, and the Resurrection of Jesus Christ.

The Pre-Millennium Position

Now, let's talk about the pre-millennium position. The position of the Pre-Millennium and the Premillennialist as to the return of Jesus and the first Resurrection and the return of Israel to her land is proven by the use of the Bible numbers.

It has been seen that the number three is connected with the Resurrection of the body. The third time the 1000 years are mentioned is in Revelation 20:1-7. It is connected with the Resurrection. "and they lived and reigned with Christ a thousand years." (Revelation 20:4)

In the next verse John referred back to this statement and said, "This is the first resurrection." (Revelation 20:5) This connects the first resurrection with the number three, the number for the Resurrection of the body.

It has been seen that eight, not three, is the number for the new birth, so this shows that the First Resurrection will be the bodily Resurrection of the Lord's people which will take place at the return of Jesus.

In Genesis 15:18, we read, "In the same day the Lord made a covenant with Abram, saying, Unto thy seed have I given this land, from the river of Egypt unto the great river Euphrates." We find the word "River" three times. This is the number for the Resurrection of the body. In this verse the name Abram occurs the 42nd time. This is the number for the coming of Jesus, and the Resurrection of the Lord's people will take place at the return of Jesus in the air. This shows that Abraham and his seed will not inherit the land under the Abrahamic covenant until after Jesus comes and the Resurrection of Abraham and the saved has taken place.

In this connection the words of Boaz to the elders are full of meaning. "Moreover Ruth the Moabitess, the wife of Mahlon, have I purchased to be my wife, to raise up the name of the dead upon his inheritance," That is found in Ruth 4:10. Here the raising up of the dead and the possession of the inheritance are connected.

This same thought is brought out by Paul in I Corinthians 15:50, "Now this I say, brethren, that flesh and blood cannot inherit the kingdom of God;" (See I Corinthians 15:50.) If you will keep in mind the subject in this chapter, we can see what Paul means. He was discussing the Resurrection of the Lord and His people, and flesh and blood cannot inherit the Kingdom of God. Then it must be resurrected or glorified people who can and will inherit the Kingdom of God. This is the typical meaning of Boaz in marrying Ruth to raise up the

161

name of the dead upon his inheritance. As Boaz was to raise up the dead upon his inheritance in a typical way, so Jesus, of which Boaz was a type, must raise up the dead in Christ before they can enter into the inheritance, because flesh and blood cannot inherit the Kingdom of God.

It is those who have a part in the First Resurrection who will live and reign with Christ 1000 years. Then it was not accidental that 42, the number for the coming of Jesus, and three, the number for the Resurrection, are found in connection with the Abramic covenant, which involved the inheritance of Canaan Land.

The third Beatitude is in keeping with the same ideal. The third Beatitude is "Blessed are the meek: for they shall inherit the earth." (Matthew 5:5) Here the number for the Resurrection of the body is connected with the saints' inheritance of the earth. This, as well as all we have already seen, puts the inheritance of the saints and their reign after the Resurrection which will be the First Resurrection.

Now let us get back to the First Resurrection. The First Resurrection is mentioned two times. It is found in Revelation 20:5-6. This number has been seen to stand for division or separation. The First Resurrection will be the separating Resurrection. It will separate the saved and the unsaved dead. It will bring the saved out of their graves to take part in the 1000-year reign. It will leave the unsaved dead in their graves to be raised 1000 years later. John said that the dead lived not again until the 1000 years were finished. In this place the expression "thousand years" occurs the fourth time.

Four is the number connected with man in his creative or natural state, hence an unsaved man. These dead will not be raised until the 1000 years are over. The Greek translation shows that there are 50 Greek letters in the statement. "But the rest of the dead lived not again until the thousand years were finished." It shows that the next statement, "This is the first Resurrection." has 20 Greek letters. (See Revelation 20:5.) When the 50 is multiplied by 20 that makes 1000, the number of years we have in this verse. The expression "the thousand years" is a translation of three Greek words which contain ten Greek letters and those letters are "TA XILIA ETA." Let's multiply these ten letters by the three words contained in them and we will get 1000. (Ten times ten times ten equals one thousand.)

In Revelation 20:4 we read these words, "and reigned with Christ a thousand years." There are four Greek words and 25 Greek letters in this statement. When 25 is multiplied by four it equals 100. The four words and 25 letters are followed by ten Greek letters translated "a thousand years." When 100 is multiplied by this ten we again get 1000. In Revelation 20:6 we read, "he that hath part in the first resurrection:" (this has ten letters). "he that hath part" has five Greek words and 20 Greek letters are in "the first resurrection." When we multiply ten and five and 20 we again get 1000.

In Westcock's text there are 47 Greek letters in the expression, "but the rest of the dead lived not again until the thousand years were finished." But reference is given to a footnote where the three-letter word "KAI" is found, and if this word was added to what I am going to give next, it would also have 50 letters, and the numbers would work out as they do in any Greek text.

In Revelation 20:1-2, we read, "And I saw an angel come down from heaven, having the key of the bottomless pit and a great chain in his hand. And he laid hold on the dragon that old serpent, which is the Devil, and Satan, and bound him a thousand years." In this statement there are 42 Greek words corresponding with the number for the coming of Christ Jesus, and showing that the devil will be bound 1000 years at the Lord's return. This puts the return of Jesus and the binding of the devil before the 1000-year reign. This is the PRE-MILLENNIUM Position.

Now, in Revelation 20:4 we read, "And I saw thrones, and they sat upon them," The Goodspeed translation reads, "power to act as judges was given to them". In this statement there are 11 Greek words and 53 Greek letters. Number 11 has been shown to stand for judgment. The 11 Greek words

163

in this statement stand for the judgment about which we read in this statement. Now, subtract 11 for judgment from 53, the number of Greek letters in this passage, and we have exactly 42, the number for the coming of Jesus, showing that at the coming of Jesus, His glorified saints will be given authority to execute judgment over the nations. "Do ye not know that the saints shall judge the world?" (See I Corinthians 6:2.) "But that which ye have already hold fast till I come." (Revelation 2:25)

Notice what follows, "And he that overcometh and keepeth my works unto the end, to him will I give power over the nations: And he shall rule them with a rod of iron;" See Revelation 2:26-28. This connects the ruling of the nations with the coming of Jesus. The number we have found connected the judgment of the saints with the coming of Jesus. I want to show the Jubilee year and the 1000-year reign. In Leviticus 25:10 we find that Israel had what is known as the jubilee year every 50 years.

In this year (Jubilee) every man returned to his own possession and his own people. Now in the concordance it shows that the Hebrew word "Yobal" translated "Jubilee" is found 20 times in the book of Leviticus. This corresponds exactly with the number of Greek letters that have been found in Revelation 20:5, and the order in which they occur in the two sentences in the verse, 50 and 20. When the 50 (years) is multiplied by 20 (the number of times the word "Yobal" translated "Jubilee"), we get exactly 1000 (years).

In every man returning to his own possession in the Jubilee year, we have the picture of Israel returning to her own land in the 1000-year reign. The MILLENNIUM AGE will be earth's great JUBILEE. Note, my children, that the word translated "Jubilee" in Leviticus 25:9 is not "Yobal" but another Hebrew word. This leaves just 20 times for the word "Jubilee" as translated "Yobal". I wanted you to know that. There is always some sceptic or doubter trying to change the Word of God.

Perpetuality of the Church

I want to talk now about the perpetuality of the Church. We have seen that the number 23 stands for death and in Matthew 16:18, we read, "And I say also unto thee, That thou art Peter, and upon this rock I will build my church; and the gates of hell shall not prevail against it." Here is a promise that the Church of the Lord Jesus would not die out. There are 23 Greek words found in this statement. This is the number for death, and Jesus assured us that the gates of Hades or death would not prevail against the church.

In Revelation 1:10-20, we have John's vision of Jesus amid the seven golden candlesticks. Jesus explained the meaning of this by saying, "The mystery of the *seven* stars which thou sawest in my right hand, and the *seven* golden candlesticks. The *seven* stars are the angels of the *seven* churches: and the *seven* candlesticks which thou sawest are the *seven* churches." Here we have the number seven said six times over. Six times seven is 42, the number connected with the coming of Jesus Christ. So the presence of Jesus Christ is found in the midst of the seven candlesticks which are the churches, guaranteeing that His church will continue until He comes again in spite of Satan's efforts to destroy it.

All right! Death is a separation, not an annihilation. Orthodox believers have always contended that death is a separation and not an annihilation or extinction of being. This position of theirs is abundantly confirmed by the Bible system of numbers. While 23 is the number for death, death itself means a separation and we have seen that the number two is connected with division or separation. Over and over again we find this number two stands for separation in connection with death. When God pronounced the sentence of death upon man, He used the word "dust" two times: "Dust thou art and to dust thou shalt return." Here the word dust is used two times. Two are mentioned in the death of Abraham. "Then Abraham gave up the ghost, and died in a good old

165

age, an old man, and full of years; and was gathered to his people. And his sons Isaac and Ishmael buried him in the cave of Machpelah, in the field of Ephron the son of Zohar the Hittite, which is before Mamre." That is Genesis 25:8, 9. In Genesis 25:1-4 it tells us about six sons which Abraham had by Keturah. He had eight sons in all, but none of these sons by Keturah are mentioned in connection with Abraham's death. Two are mentioned in connection with Isaac. It says in Genesis 35:29, "And Isaac gave up the ghost, and died, and was gathered unto his people, being old and full of days; and his sons Esau and Jacob buried him."

It states, "Joseph commanded his servants the physicians to embalm his father: and the physicians embalmed Israel." Had we been writing this no doubt we would have said, "And Joseph commanded the physicians to embalm his father and they did so," but that would not have created the numerology of the passage and that is why I am absolutely against any revised edition of the King James version of the Holy Bible that it is not word for word according to the Greek translation of the Holy Bible and would change all the meaning of the numeral system.

Many times the nouns are repeated when it seems unnecessary and when it seems that the use of a pronoun would have been better; but what may seem to man an unnecessary repetition is employed to bring out the numeral value of the passage. I believe that Greeks were great writers. So the writing in Greek, I believe to be done by the authority of God.

Just before his death Joseph spoke to his people two times: "And Joseph said unto his brethren, I die: and God will surely visit you, and bring you out of this land unto the land which he sware to Abraham, to Isaac and to Jacob. And Joseph took an oath of the children of Israel, saying, God will surely visit you, and ye shall carry up my bones from hence." (Genesis 50:24, 25) That is twice. Rebecca's nurse is mentioned twice in the Bible. She is mentioned first in Genesis 24:59, and the second time in Genesis 35:18 where we read about her death.

In Genesis 46:12, we read about the sons of Judah. It is said, "Er and Onam died in the land of Canaan." See Genesis 46:12. In Leviticus 10:1-2, we read about the death of two of Aaron's sons, Nadab and Abihu. In Judges 7:25 we read, "And they took two princes of the Midianites, Oreb and Zeeb, and they slew Oreb upon the rock Oreb, and Zeeb they slew at the winepress of Zeeb," Here again two are connected with death. In Ruth 1:5 we read, "And Mahlon and Chilion died also both of them;" Again we have two connected with death.

In II Samuel 3:30 we read, "So Joab and Abishai his brother slew Abner, because he had slain their brother Asahel at Gibeon in the battle." Again we have two connected with death.

In Esther 2:21 we read where "two of the king's chamberlains, Bigthan and Teresh," sought to put King Ahasuerus to death. In Isaiah 37:37, 38 we read where Sennacherib was killed by two of his sons.

When Jesus received the news of the sickness of Lazarus He abode two days still in the place where He was. Then He told His disciples that Lazarus was dead. See John 11:1-14.

When Dorcas or Tabitha died, the disciples sent two men after the Apostle Peter. See Acts 9:36-38. In I Timothy 5:6, the word "liveth" is used twice with the word "dead." "But she that liveth in pleasure is dead while she liveth." In Revelation 11:13, the word "earthquake" is used twice in connection with death. "And the same hour was there a great earthquake, and the tenth part of the city fell, and in the earthquake were slain of men seven thousand:" Other places could be given where the number two is connected with death. Since number two stands for separation or division this shows that death is a separation.

Some Amazing Examples of the Numerical Design

I would like to give you some amazing examples that Jesus, my Lord, gave me. They are found in the New Testament which should help you in studying the Bible, the Holy Book, the King James Version finished in 1611. Jesus told me that this is the true Book of God's Word, the only book that will work out in the true numerical design because it truly came by God, Jesus Christ, our Lord, unto man by no private interpretation, so let us start first with —

Luke 13:16

"And ought not this woman, being a daughter of Abraham, whom Satan hath bound, lo, these eighteen years, be loosed from this bond on the Sabbath day?"

This passage has been quoted before but only briefly discussed. In this passage there are exactly 25 Greek words. The woman was bound 18 years and loosed from her bond on the Sabbath Day, which was the seventh day of the week. When seven is added to 18 that makes 25, the exact number of Greek words in the passage. Number 25 stands for the forgiveness of sins. When one's sins are forgiven, he is loosed from the bond of Satan.

Number 18 stands for bondage. The woman was in bondage 18 years. The words, "lo, these eighteen years," have just 18 Greek letters. The woman was loosed on the seventh day. The Greek word for "be loosed" has seven letters. The number seven stands for completeness. When Jesus forgives a person's sins and sets him free from Satan's bond, he is forgiven of all his sins. "And you, being dead in your sins and the uncircumcision of your flesh, hath he quickened together with him, having forgiven you ALL *TRESPASSES*;" (Colossians 2:13)

168

When the Lord saves, He completely saves. When Jesus cast the unclean spirit out of a child, He said, "I charge thee, come out of him, and enter no more into him." (Mark 9:25) The passage from Greek reads as such (Mark 9:25): "And no more mayest thou enter into him." This passage has five Greek words and 25 Greek letters. Here is the number for forgiveness of sins, and grace. We find that 25 added to five is 30, which stands for the blood which we are covered with for salvation, and to purify our saved condition.

Here Is Another Amazing Example: John 3:18

"But he that believeth not, already has been judged, because he hath not believed in the name of the only begotten Son of God."

This passage shall be examined according to the Greek text and translation. The passage shall be divided into three parts and each part examined separately, and then the passage looked at as a whole by revelation through the power of the Holy Ghost which is the power and presence of Jesus the Christ, our Lord and God.

In the words, "he that believeth not," there are four Greek words and 13 Greek letters. Four has been found by Jesus' own words to represent the natural or unsaved man. Who will say the unbeliever is not an unsaved man? Number 13 stands for sin, and shows the sin of unbelief the man is in. The words, "already, has been judged," have two Greek words and 11 Greek letters.

Number two stands for separation, and number 11 stands for judgment. The passage says the man has already been judged. Unbelief separates the man from God. When the two words in this part of the quotation are added to the 11 letters, they total 13, which stands for sin and is the exact number of letters found in "But he that believeth not," When the two words in "already has been judged," are added to the four Greek words in "But he that believeth not", we have six words altogether. Six is Satan's number, and the unbeliever is under the influence of Satan. "If our gospel be hid, it is hid to them that are lost: In whom the god of this world [the devil] hath blinded the minds of them which believe not," (I Corinthians 4:3-4)

So the unbeliever is under the influence of Satan even as the six words in "he that believeth not already ha., been judged" shows us. Then the last part of the quotation, "because he hath not believed in the name of the only begotten Son of God," has 11 Greek words. Eleven is the number for JUDGMENT, and it shows why the man has to be judged. This number of words equals the number of letters in "already has been judged." When the 11 words in this part of the quotation are added to the four in the first part and the two in the second part, they total 17 words in all.

This equals in number the four words plus the 13 letters in the first part of the quotation, "But he that believeth not," So the number of letters in the first part plus the words in the first part equals all the words in the whole quotation. The number of letters plus the number of words in the second part equals the number of letters in the first part. The number of letters in the second part equals the number of words in the third part, and the number of letters plus the number of words in the first part equals the number of words in the whole quotation. The 17 words in the whole quotation show that the man has already been overcome by sin and Satan.

Colossians 1:13-14

"Who hath delivered us from the power of darkness, and hath translated us into the Kingdom of his dear Son: In whom we have redemption through his blood, even the forgiveness of sins."

This is the disputed passage, the one over which there has been so much controversy since the new Revised Version has come out. God has the words "through his blood," in His text. Brother Don, who received his revelation through Jesus, shall now prove with the use of Bible numbers that the words "through his blood" are from the Greek word "APOLU-TROSIS" which Thayer says means "to let go" or "set free by paying a price."

First of all we have man in a condition of servitude or bondage when he is under the power of darkness. As such he stood in need of someone to pay the price for his release from this bondage. In the words, "Who hath delivered us from the power of darkness, and hath translated us into the kingdom of his dear Son:" we have 18 Greek words. We have seen that 18 stands for bondage. In these 18 words there is seen a picture of the bondage from which the saved are set free. In the words "In whom we have redemption" there are 23 letters (23 is the number for death), showing that in our redemption from the power of darkness we have also been redeemed from death.

The words "we have redemption" have 20 Greek letters, and 20 has been found to be the number for redemption. The words "through his blood" have 18 Greek letters. This equals the number of the words, "Who hath delivered us from the power of darkness, and hath translated us into the kingdom of his dear Son." It is the number for bondage, and shows the price that was paid by which we were redeemed or set free from a condition of bondage.

The statement, "In whom we have redemption through his blood, the forgiveness of sins" (even is left out because it was added by man), has 13 Greek words, and 13 has been seen to be the number for sin, and the 13th word in this statement is "sins". Leave out the statement, "through his blood", and the numerology and truth of the passage is marred. The Lord Jesus certainly had a purpose in giving us this number system. He said it will prove my Word to be truth and no man can change the truth by adding or removing a word from God's own Word. Who knows but what He gave it to us for just such a time as this, when man has brought forth not less than 267 denominations in the United States that are not men-

171

tioned in the Holy Bible. He has so arranged His Word that His people can check up on those who would corrupt or take away from His word by scriptural adultery. Brother Don is aware of the fact that the Weslcott-Hart text omits the words "through his blood". Jesus told me the King James Version is the text to go by, that it will withstand the numerology of the number system and was brought forth by the Inspiration of God. The King James has it, and the numerology of the passage shows that it belongs to the passage. Brother Don has examined many texts of the Bible from Greek and Hebrew, but Jesus told me that only the King James will work out in the numbering system for truth.

Ephesians 2:8

"For by grace are ye saved through faith; and that not of yourselves: it is the gift of God."

In the translation Jesus, my God, gave me, the statement, "For by grace are ye saved through faith;" has eight Greek words and 38 Greek letters. Eight stands for the New Birth, which those who are saved have. Thirty-eight stands for righteousness, and those who have been saved by God's grace have been made righteous.

In the statement, "For by grace are ye saved through faith;" we have GRACE and SALVATION and FAITH. The number for Grace is five. The number for Salvation is 14. The number for Faith is 19. When these numbers, five and 14 and 19, are added, they equal 38, the exact number of Greek letters in the statement, "For by grace are ye saved through faith;" The words, "and that not of yourselves: it is the Gift of God:" have 28 letters; 28 is the number for eternal life, and we are told by the Word of God that "the gift of God is eternal life" (Romans 6:23) and the one who has been saved by God's grace has eternal life.

I Thessalonians 4:14

"For if we believe that Jesus died and rose again, even so them also which sleep in Jesus will God bring with him."

There are 91 Greek letters in this passage. In this passage we have under consideration the death and resurrection of Jesus, the death of the saints, the second coming of Jesus, and the coming forth of the saved dead.

When we add 23 for the death of Jesus, three for His resurrection, 23 again for the death of the saints and 42 for the coming of Jesus, the total is 91, the exact number of Greek letters in the passage. Number 91 we have found to be the number for "CASTING OUT." In this connection, let us consider Isaiah 26:19, "Awake and sing, ye that dwell in the dust: for thy dew is as the dew of herbs, and the earth shall CAST OUT THE DEAD." Number 91, the number found to be connected with CASTING OUT, is found in I Thessalonians 4:14.

When Jesus comes, the earth shall cast out the bodies of the sleeping saints who shall awake and sing. It takes the number connected with the death of Jesus, the number for His resurrection, the number for the death of the saints, and the number for the coming of Jesus to add up to 91, the number of letters found in this passage. And it will take all these things to cause the earth to cast out the bodies of the sleeping saints at the coming of Christ.

Matthew 1:21

"And she shall bring forth a son, and thou shalt call his name JESUS: for he shall save his people from their sins."

In the verse quoted above, Jesus showed me there is an amazing example of Bible numbers which will baffle the combined wisdom of the modernistic world, and which this writer, Brother Don, challenges the combined wisdom of the

173

world to answer.

In the statement, "And she shall bring forth a son, and thou shalt call his Name, JESUS:" there are 42 Greek letters, and nine Greek words. Just four verses above this passage we are shown that there were 42 generations from Abraham to the coming of Christ. (Matthew 1:17)

Number nine has been shown to be connected with the fruit of the Spirit. Count the words in Galatians 5:22-23. There we find listed nine things as the FRUIT of the Spirit. When the angel of the Lord told Mary that she should conceive and bring forth a son, she asked, "How shall this be, seeing I know not a man?" The angel answered her by saying, "The Holy Ghost shall come upon thee, and the power of the Highest shall overshadow thee:" See Luke 1:26-35. The nine words in the statement, "And she shall bring forth a son, and thou shalt call his name JESUS:" show to us the part the Holy Spirit had in the conception and birth of Jesus, since nine is the number connected with the FRUIT of the Spirit. Here the miraculous conception and birth of Jesus, and the fact that it was brought about by the Spirit of God, is not only plainly stated in the Scriptures, but the same is connected with the influence of the Spirit. The number of letters (42) corresponds exactly with the number of generations from Abraham to Christ, as shown by Matthew 1:17.

Now let us study the last part of the verse, and then the whole verse, or the two parts together, and we will find something to make us marvel indeed. The last part of this verse states, "for he shall save his people from their sins." There are 44 Greek letters in this statement. It says that, "he shall save his people." Number 14 has been found to be the number for SALVATION, and 30 stands for THE BLOOD OF CHRIST which saves. These two numbers, 14 and 30, add up to 44, the number of Greek letters in this statement.

In the whole verse there are 86 Greek letters, and 19 words. Number 19 has been seen to be the number for FAITH, and the Bible teaches that we are saved by Grace through FAITH. So the ones whom Jesus saves are those who have FAITH. Now let us add the 19 words to the 86 letters, and we will get 105. The verse says that "he shall save his people from their sins." When we take 14, the number for SALVATION, and add all the numbers from one up to 14, we get 105, the exact number we get when we add the 42 letters, the 44 letters, and the 19 words.

Now let us subtract instead of add those 19 words to the number of letters in the verse and we will get the same thing in a slightly different way. Nineteen subtracted from 86 leaves 67. This is 42 for the coming of Christ, which is in this verse, and 25 for the Forgiveness of Sins. The verse says, "He shall save His people from their sins." When one's sins have been forgiven he has been saved from his sins, so the result is the same either way we run these numbers.

It has been shown by Jesus that the 42 letters, 44 letters and the 19 words add up to 105. The passage says, "he shall save HIS PEOPLE from their sins." HIS PEOPLE are the ELECTION OF GRACE.

Number 100 has been related by Jesus to stand for the ELECT and five has been related to be the number for GRACE. When the 100 and the five are added, they make 105, the number we get by adding the number of letters in the verse to the number of words in the same.

Hebrews 11:30

"By faith the walls of Jericho fell down, after they were compassed about seven days."

Jesus related the translation from Greek to be "For seven days." The Greek for the words "For seven days" is "epi epta ameras." Let the reader count these letters and he will find that they are 13 in number. By turning back to Joshua 6:3-4, he will find that the children of Israel compassed the walls of Jericho once a day for six days and then seven times on the seventh day. This makes 13 times they went around the wall, which is the exact number of

Greek letters found in "For seven days."

Matthew 27:6

There are exactly 30 Greek letters in the statement, "And the chief priest took the silver pieces," This was the exact number of pieces of silver for which Judas betrayed Jesus, and which he had returned and had cast down. See Matthew 27:3-5. How will the doubter and the modernist account for all these things unless they accept the truth of Divine inspiration?

The Raising of Lazarus

In the raising of Lazarus from the dead there is one of the most wonderful and soul-stirring examples of the numerical design in the Bible. I shall quote this passage as translated by Jesus the Word, and then give what is found in the numerical pattern.

John 11:43-45

"And when he thus had spoken, he cried with a loud voice, Lazarus, come forth. And he that was dead came forth, bound hand and foot with graveclothes: and his face was bound about with a napkin. Jesus saith unto them, Loose him, and let him go. Then many of the Jews which came to Mary, and had seen the things which Jesus did, believed on him."

Here we have set forth the account of the RESURRECTION of Lazarus. In the words, "Lazarus, come forth," there are three English words and three Greek words. This is the number for the Resurrection, and with these three words, Jesus brought about the Resurrection of Lazarus. The THIRD one of these words has three Greek letters. In the three words there are 14 Greek letters. This is the number for

176

salvation or deliverance, and at this time the body of Lazarus was saved or delivered from death and the grave, at least for a time.

When the three words are added to the 14 letters, that makes 17 (the number for VICTORY); Lazarus had the victory over the grave. When we multiply 14, the number of the letters, by three, the number of words, that makes 42, which is the number for the Coming of Christ. Jesus had said to His disciples, "Our friend Lazarus sleepeth; but I go, that I may awake him out of sleep." (John 11:11) So here He has come to awaken Lazarus. When Jesus comes back again, He will awake His saints out of their rest, and they, like Lazarus, will have their bodies saved and they will have victory over death and the grave.

Just after Jesus said, "Lazarus, come forth", we read, "And he that was dead came forth, bound hand and foot with graveclothes, and his face was bound about with a napkin." In this statement there are 17 Greek words; this equals the number of words plus the number of letters in "Lazarus come forth." This again expresses the victory which Lazarus had over the grave. The 17 (three words and 14 letters) in "Lazarus come forth" shows the victory unto which Jesus was calling Lazarus. The 17 words that follow the words "Lazarus come forth" show the victory that Lazarus actually had when he came out of the grave.

Now add the three words, "Lazarus come forth," to the 17 words that follow, and we get 20, which is the number for redemption. Here we have Lazarus redeemed from the grave.

After Lazarus had come forth, Jesus said to them, "Loose him and let [him, understood, but not in the Greek] go." Here Jesus used five words in the original language. They loosed what was bound. His two feet, his two hands, and his face (one) were the things bound, and the things loosed. Thus the number of words Jesus used here equals the things bound, and the things that were loosed.

In the five Greek words, "Loose him, and let go", we have five words and 26 letters. Number five is for GRACE that looses or sets free. Number 26 stands for the Gospel. In Acts 20:24, Paul called the gospel, "the gospel of the GRACE of God." Here we have death and the resurrection under consideration, and the gospel concerns Christ's death for our sins, and His resurrection, and also the good news of our coming resurrection. The resurrection of Lazarus was good news.

When Lazarus died, they bound his feet, his hands, and his face in preparing him for burial. We have seen that number 23 stands for death. In the words, "the foot", "the Hand" and "the Face", there are exactly 23 Greek letters. (The definite article "the" is not used in the translation, yet it occurs before each of these words in the original language, giving us exactly 23 letters.)

I have pointed out by the help of my God, Jesus, that there are five Greek words and 26 Greek letters in the words, "Loose him, and let go." Here are the numbers for GRACE and the GOSPEL; and GRACE and the GOSPEL bring about FAITH in the hearts of men. "faith cometh by hearing, and hearing by the word of God." (Romans 10:17)

Immediately following these five words and 26 letters which Jesus spoke, we read, "Then many of the Jews which came to Mary, and had seen the things which Jesus did, believed on him." Here is FAITH brought about by death and the Resurrection. The number for FAITH is 19 and there are 19 Greek words in this statement.

Now let us sum up what has been found in these three verses. We have seen set forth in numbers the doctrine of the Resurrection, the Salvation of the Body by deliverance, Victory over the Grave, the Coming of Christ, Redemption, Grace, the Gospel, Death and Faith. Where in the writings of men can anything be found that can begin to compare with this? What a task an uninspired man would be up against trying to write a short passage like this one, setting forth the thoughts that are contained in this short passage, and then making the number of his words and letters count out to fit the number system as they do here. Truly the Bible is the miracle of the ages!

But we are not yet through with this passage. This writer, Brother Don, has one more thing to point out in connection with this passage, and it will show a beautiful picture of the time when the saints of God will close their earthly life and their stay in the grave. Commencing with the words Jesus spoke to Lazarus when He raised him, "Lazarus, come forth", and ending with the statement, "let him go", we have exactly 29 Greek words, and 29 is the number we have found by the revelation of Jesus to stand for DEPARTURE. The 29th word is "go". No doubt when Lazarus was let go he DEPARTED from the mouth of that grave to be with Jesus Who had raised him from the dead. Even so, when Christ comes from the gates of heaven with a shout (even as He spoke to Lazarus with a LOUD VOICE), and calls His saints from the graves where they are resting, then they shall come forth from the graves and DEPART TO BE WITH CHRIST. Whose soul would not be thrilled by such a picture as this?

Then, as Lazarus had the VICTORY over the grave, we too shall have the victory, and can sing, "O death, where is thy sting? O grave, where is thy victory? The sting of death is sin; and the strength of sin is the Law. But thanks be to God, which giveth us the Victory through our Lord Jesus Christ." (I Corinthians 15:55-57)

Infinite Wisdom and Power of God

Now, I want to go into the Infinite Wisdom and Power of God. Who can study these things and question the fact that God is infinite in His knowledge and power? The numbers of the Bible prove without a doubt that the Birth, Lives, experiences and Death of Bible Characters was in the mind of God before the world existed. If it had not been, then the numbers connected with their birth and deaths and other incidents of their lives would never have fitted into their numeral pattern of the Scriptures as they do.

It has been seen that Jacob was 15 years old at the death of his grandfather, Abraham, and 120 years old at the death of his father, Isaac. It has also been seen that when all the numbers from one to 15 are added, the total is 120, corresponding with the age of Jacob at the death of his father. God had to control the time of these men and the time of the death of Abraham and Isaac to make things work out like this.

It has been seen that Abraham was 99 years old when he was circumcised, and that Ishmael was 13 years old and Isaac was eight days old. It has also been shown that all the numbers from one to 13 add up to 91 and that when the number eight, which was the number connected with the circumcision of Isaac, is added to this number, we get 99, the exact number connected with the circumcision of Abraham.

God has to time the birth as well as the time of their circumcision of all these to make a number work out in this way. Had Abraham been 98 years old and Ishmael 12 years old, the numbers would not have worked out as they do. Thus we can see that all these things were fashioned by God and woven into His numeral design from the beginning. We have also seen how we get 91 when we add the numbers of the months the beast will be in power, 42, and the number of times the beast is mentioned, which is 36, and the number of times the word "Dragon" occurs in the book of Revelation, which is 13.

Part of the same numeral design is seen in this as well in the life and circumcision of Ishmael. We have also seen that Paul used the word "Faith" 19 times in his discussion of justification of Faith, and we have seen that it was Faith that made the birth of Isaac possible. "Through faith also Sarah herself received strength to conceive seed, and was delivered of a child when she was past age, because she judged him faithful who had promised." (Hebrews 11:11) There are ex-

180

actly 19 (the number for Faith) Greek words in this statement, and when all the numbers from one to 19 are added, they total 190. In Genesis 17:1-24 and Genesis 21:5, we learn that the combined ages of Abraham and Sarah at the birth of Isaac are 190 years. Part of this pattern is found in the Old Testament, and part is found in the New Testament. When they are brought together, the different parts fit together to form the perfect picture.

This not only shows that these things were in the mind of God from the beginning; but it shows His infinite Power and control over all things, even the ones who put the Holy Bible together, making them work out to fit the numeral design that was in His mind from the beginning. No wonder Paul exclaimed, "O the depth of the riches both of the wisdom and knowledge of God. how unsearchable are his judgments, and his ways past finding out!" See Romans 11:33.

These things also prove that the God of the Jewish scriptures is also the God of the New Testament scriptures. Here is a challenge to every Jew. Here is proof that Jesus of Nazareth is the Messiah for whom he is looking because the New Testament plainly declares Him to be such. The Samaritan woman said to Him, "The woman saith unto him, I know that Messias cometh, which is called Christ: when he is come, he will tell us all things. Jesus saith unto her, I that speak unto thee am he." That's John 4:25, 26.

It has been shown that there were 276 on the ship on which Paul sailed who were threatened with death. I have also shown that Paul, upon the authority of God's Word said they would all be saved from death. I have also shown that they were saved from the storm and the sea on the 14th day. The Bible bears this out in Acts 27:27-44. When 12, the number for Divine Authority, is divided into 276, you get exactly 23, the number for death. When all the numbers from one to 23 are added we again get 276, the number of men on the ship and the number saved from death. The 14th day on which they were saved from death corresponds with the number we have found for Salvation, and that is 14.

In order for these numbers to work out like they do, God had to see that exactly 276 men, no more, no less, got on that ship. He had to control the wind and the waves, the drift of the ship, to make it land on that island on the 14th day of the storm.

The numerology of this passage corresponds exactly with the numeral patterns that we have found in God's mind from the beginning. Who can read these things in the Word of God without being overpowered by the infinite wisdom and power of the Eternal God, the Father, Jesus Christ of Nazareth? In all these things we can see God's knowledge, His infinite wisdom and power, His divine purpose, His predestination, His rule of Providence. Where can anything be found that can compare with all this? Before such wisdom and power let men humble themselves in the dust of the earth, and acknowledge the infinite wisdom and power of God, Jesus Christ, the Father Almighty. Hallelujah! Thank You, Jesus!

Combination of Numeral Pattern of Abraham's Family

I want to close out this work in this book with a combination of the numeral pattern of Abraham's family. I am going to finish this book with 17 combinations.

The numeral pattern that is interwoven into Abraham's family is enough to convince the most hardened sceptic of the Bible of the truth of Divine Inspiration and Interpretation. The three numbers connected with the circumcision at the time when circumcision was performed can be used to show all the numbers connected with the lives and deaths of the members of Abraham's family.

Let's take the first number connected with circumcision. In Genesis 17:24, we find that Abraham was 99 years old when he was circumcised. Since he was 75 when he came to

Canaan (see Genesis 12:4, 5), he was circumcised 24 years after coming to Canaan.

In Genesis 17:25, it is stated that his son Ishmael was 13 years old when circumcised and in Genesis 17:26, it says that this was the same day that Abraham was circumcised.

In Genesis 21:4, it is stated that Abraham circumcised his son Isaac when he was eight days old. Since Abraham was 100 years old when Isaac was born (Genesis 21:5), this took place 25 years after Abraham came to Canaan. The three numbers connected with circumcision shall be this: Abraham, 99 years; Ishmael, 13 years; and Isaac, eight days. Now the next combination: it has already been shown that the numbers from one to 13 add up to 91, and when eight, the number connected with Isaac's circumcision, is added to 91, the sum is 99, the number connected with Abraham's circumcision.

The product of the numbers connected with Ishmael and Isaac, 13 and eight, is 104; eight times 13 is 104. The difference between the two numbers eight and 13 is five. When five is subtracted from 104 the remainder is 99, the number for Abraham's circumcision. The sum of the numbers connected with the circumcision of Abraham and Ishmael, 99 and 13, is 112; 99 plus 13 is 112. When 112 is divided by eight, the number connected with Isaac's circumcision, the answer is 14, which was the age of Ishmael when Isaac was born. See Genesis 16:16.

We learn that Abraham was 86 when Ishmael was born and, in Genesis 21:5, we learn that he was 100 when Isaac was born. So the difference in the ages of the two sons was 14 years. When 14 is added to 86, the total is 100, the age of Abraham when Isaac was born.

Let's take the fourth combination: Isaac died at the age of 180 years. See Genesis 35:28, 29. He was eight days old when circumcised. All the numbers from one to eight add up to 36. The difference between the numbers connected with the circumcision of Isaac and Ishmael, 13 and eight, is five. When 36 is multiplied by five, the product is 180, which was

Isaac's age when he died.

Let's take the fifth combination: Sarah was ten years younger than Abraham. (Genesis 17:17) Since Abraham was 75 when he came to Canaan, Sarah was 65 at that time. When 13, the number connected with Ishmael's circumcision, is multiplied by five, the difference between 13 and eight, connected with the circumcision of Ishmael and Isaac, the product is 65, the age of Sarah when she came to Canaan.

Let's try the sixth combination: when eight, the number connected with Isaac's circumcision, is multiplied by five, the difference between 13 and eight, the product is 40. When all the numbers from one to eight are added, the sum is 36 as shown, and the sum of 40 and 36 is 76. Since Abraham was 86 when Ishmael was born, then 76 was Sarah's age when Ishmael was born.

Let's take the seventh combination: when the number 76, found in the combination that I just gave, is added to 99, the number connected with Abraham's circumcision, the sum is 175, which was the age of Abraham when he died. (Genesis 25:7, 8)

The eighth combination: Abraham was 100 and Sarah was 90 years old when Isaac was born. (Genesis 21:5; Genesis 17:17) So the combined ages of the two parents at Isaac's birth were 190 years. Ishmael was circumcised when 13 years of age, and all the numbers from one to 13 add up to 91. When 99, the number connected with Abraham's circumcision, is added to 91, the sum is 190, the combined ages of Sarah and Abraham when Isaac was born.

The ninth combination: Ishmael was circumcised when 13, and when all the numbers from one to 13 are added, they will total 91. Number eight was connected with Isaac's circumcision and all the numbers from one to eight add up to 36. When 91 and 36 are added, the sum is 127, which was the age of Sarah when she died. (Genesis 23:1, 2)

The tenth combination: Isaac was circumcised 20 years after Abraham came to Canaan. When this number is added to 91 and 13, the numbers connected with the circumcision of Abraham and Ishmael, the sum is 137. This was the age of Ishmael when he died. (Genesis 25:17)

The 11th combination: Ishmael was born 11 years after Abraham came into Canaan. The numbers 99 and 13, connected with the circumcision of Abraham and Ishmael, add up to 112. Number eight was connected with Isaac's circumcision and all the numbers from one to eight add up to 36. One hundred and twelve plus 36 adds up to 148, which was the number of years from the time Abraham came into Canaan until the death of Ishmael.

Let's take the 12th combination: when eight, the number connected with Isaac's circumcision, is multiplied by five, the product is 40. All the numbers from one to eight add up to 36. Numbers 40 and 36 add up to 86. When we add 24, the number of years Abraham had been in Canaan, to 76, the sum is 100, which was Abraham's age when Isaac was born.

The 13th combination: when 14, the age of Ishmael at Isaac's birth, is added to 40 and 36, the number found in the combination I just gave you, the sum is 90, which was Sarah's age when Isaac was born.

The 14th combination: the difference in the ages of Ishmael and Isaac was 14 years. The difference between their ages at the time of their circumcision is 13 and eight, which is five. When five is added to 14, the difference in the ages of the two sons, the sum is 19, the number that has been seen to stand for faith. Abraham was ten years older than Sarah. When 19 is multiplied by ten, the product is 190, the combined ages of Abraham and Sarah when Isaac was born.

Let's take the 15th one: the three numbers connected with the circumcision, 99, 13 and eight, add up to 120. This was Jacob's age when Isaac died. (Genesis 35:28, 29) It is stated that Isaac was 180 years old when he died. In Genesis 25:26, it is stated that Isaac was 60 years old when Jacob was born. So Isaac died when Jacob was 120 years old, the number found by adding the three numbers connected with the circumcision.

Let's take the 16th combination: Abraham was 100 years

of age when Isaac was born; Isaac was 60 years old when Jacob was born, and Abraham was 160 years old when Jacob was born. Since Abraham was 170 years old when he died, then Jacob was 15 years old when Abraham died. The three numbers connected with circumcision, 99, 13, and eight, add up to 120. When divided by eight, the number connected with Isaac's circumcision, the result is 15, which was Jacob's age when Abraham died.

Let's take the 17th and final combination: Jacob was 15 when Abraham died, and 120 when Isaac died. All the numbers from one to 15 add up to 120, the age of Jacob when Isaac died. I could give you almost 100 combinations of numbers connected with Abraham's family which work out the same way. The numbers and times that the names of Abraham, Sarah, Ishmael, and Hager occur, and the connection in which they occur, can be found in Genesis 16:16.

In this verse, Abraham was 86 and his name occurs the 55th time. The name of Hagar occurs the seventh time in the verse and Ishmael's name occurs the third time. Sarah is ten years younger than Abraham; she is 76 at this time. The numbers fit together in two ways to get Sarah's age at this time: one way to get Abraham's age, two ways to get the number of offspring. Ishmael was the offspring of Abram and Hagar. The numbers for love, bondage, judgment, and sin are found. Number seven, for the seventh time Hagar's name occurs, and three, for the third time Ishmael's name occurs, add up to ten, for the law. The numbers from one to ten add up to 55, which is the number of times Abraham's name occurs. Nothing short of a Divine mind could have the numbers arranged and placed so that they would work out in such a way. Oh, children of God, nothing short of an infinite power could have controlled the times of the births, deaths, and other happenings in the lives of these people in a way to make the numbers connected with the same fit together in such a fashion! So, yours truly, Brother Don Kistler, will close this work of numbers with the confidence that the evidence of Divine Inspiration of the Bible that is presented here can never be matched. May the doubter give up his doubt and the sceptic cease from his scorning and put his faith in God, the one God, Jesus Christ of Nazareth, and make preparations to meet Him in peace when he is summoned to the presence of Jesus Christ, God, Father Almighty, and Who is to come shortly.

My children of God, Hallelujah! I write this the eighth day of April in the year of our Lord 1971 A.D. Thank You, Jesus, may glory be unto His precious Name until His coming. Jesus, the only name I know under Heaven! All things shall be done in His Name, Jesus. I did this work by His inspiration and through His salvation given unto me, by listening to God's Word, Jesus Christ, through my own ears. I close with love and glory unto God, Jesus Christ of Nazareth, Who is the Author and Finisher of our salvation. Amen! Hallelujah! Praise His precious Holy Name!